managing

God's

money

Tyndale House Publishers, Inc.
Carol Stream, Illinois

RANDY ALCORN

Visit Tyndale's exciting Web site at www.tyndale.com.

TYNDALE and Tyndale's quill logo are registered trademarks of Tyndale House Publishers, Inc.

Managing God's Money: A Biblical Guide

Designed by Daniel Farrell

Library of Congress Cataloging-in-Publication Data

Alcorn, Randy C.
   Managing God's money : a biblical guide / Randy Alcorn.
     p. cm.
   ISBN 978-1-4143-4553-6 (sc)
   1. Christian stewardship. 2. Christian stewardship—Biblical teaching. I. Title.
   BV772.A43 2011
   248'.6--dc22   2010044879

Printed in the United States of America

17	16	15	14	13	12	11
7	6	5	4	3	2	1

I dedicate this book to some brothers who have long been Kingdom influencers through financial stewardship and giving.

Just as I honor my precious wife, Nanci, for walking with me for decades in the path of stewardship and giving, the men below who are married would give tribute to their wives, many of whom I haven't had the privilege of meeting. (Those I do know typically outclass their husbands!)

I am also aware that many other women (Nancy Leigh DeMoss and Sharon Epps among them) deserve to be on this list. So do countless men and women of every tribe, nation, and language. Unfortunately, my knowledge and memory and the space in this book are all limited, so I'm sorry to all those I should have included but didn't; God knows who you are.

Some of these brothers are living with Jesus; most are still serving him here today:

R. G. LeTourneau, Art DeMoss, Larry Burkett, Bill Bright, Stanley Tam, John Edmund Haggai, Ron Blue, Howard Dayton, Gene Getz, Tony Cimmarrusti, Daryl Heald, Todd Harper, Hugh Maclellan, Peb Jackson, Jess Correll, Alan Barnhart, Brian Kluth, Scott Preissler, Paul Meyer, Chuck Bentley, Tom Conway, Jerry Schriver, Dick Towner, Al Mueller, Forrest Reinhardt, Chris Duncan, Todd Peterson, Dave Hannah, Scott Lewis, Jay Link, Lee Jenkins, Fred Smith, Wes Wilmer, Craig Blomberg, Gary Hoag, Scott Rodin, Ray Lyne, Ralph Douderas, Jerry Caven, Don Christensen, and last but not least

David Wills, who suggested to me nearly twenty years ago, after the publication of the original Money, Possessions, and Eternity, *that I should write a smaller stewardship book like this one.*

Okay, here it is; I decided not to rush it.

Contents

Section V | Wisely Handling God's Money and Possessions

Section VI | Passing the Baton of Wise Stewardship

Introduction

OUR PERSPECTIVE on money and possessions—and how we handle them—lies at the very heart of the Christian life. Does that sound like an overstatement? It's not. The Bible emphatically demonstrates that how we view our money and possessions is of utmost importance. What we do with them will influence eternity.

The title of this book, *Managing God's Money*, is not some cute, figurative expression. It's a precise depiction of what the Bible says we are—God's money managers.

Jesus told his disciples, "There was a rich man whose manager was accused of wasting his possessions. So he called him in and asked him, 'What is this I hear about you? Give an account of your management, because you cannot be manager any longer'" (Luke 16:1-2, NIV).

This parable, like the other "stewardship parables" (see chapter 3), shows that God, who is infinitely rich and owns all things, has assigned to human beings management responsibilities over his assets. We can manage his money and possessions well, or—as in the case of this man—poorly. One day we will stand before God and give an account of how we have managed what belongs to him. Have we taken good care of it, using it wisely for purposes he approves of? Or have we misused or wasted it?

Now, it might seem unfair that we won't formally answer to God for our work as his asset managers until our lives here are done and it's too late to implement changes based on his performance review.

But it's *not* unfair. Why? Because God has recorded in the Bible everything we need to know about his investment priorities, his high standards of management, and the rewards he offers his faithful stewards.

God's Word is his Kingdom manifesto, his investment manual, and his code of business ethics. When we stand before him at the end of our lives, suppose we say, "But, God, you didn't tell me this all belonged to you; you didn't say it was my job to do with it what you wanted me to; you never told me how to conduct my business; and you never made clear which investments you considered important." He would need only to lift up the Bible and reply, "Yes I did; you simply didn't pay attention."

That's why the pages of *Managing God's Money* contain a great deal of Scripture. God's words are far more valuable than anything I have to say because he is, after all, the Creator and Owner of the universe. He promises, "[My word] shall not return to me empty, but it shall accomplish that which I purpose, and shall succeed in the thing for which I sent it" (Isaiah 55:11, ESV). God does not make that promise about your words or my words or the words of any investment guru, but only about *his* Word.

This book won't tell you how to achieve your financial goals, but it will provide the light in which your financial goals should be formulated. That's why the central focus of this book is not insurance but *assurance*, not securities but *security*, not trusts but *trust*, not principal but *principles*, not real estate but *real* estate.

You will not find any net-worth calculations (which we easily mistake for self-worth calculations), but you will see how God measures your life's worth. You won't find advice about tax shelters, IRA contributions, or choosing between term and whole-life insurance. There is a place for such things—but only after a close look at what God has to say about money. *That* is the purpose of this book.

So where are we headed in *Managing God's Money*? Turn back and look through the table of contents, and you'll see not only section and chapter titles but also headings within chapters. These will give you a clear picture of the book's contents.

You may skip forward to a chapter of particular interest, say, on eternal rewards, tithing, lifestyle, debt, or retirement. But keep in mind that much of the biblical foundation for how to approach those areas has been laid earlier in the book. Every section and chapter builds on previous ones, and whether you go through this as an individual or as a group, you'll experience the greatest benefit if you read it sequentially.

When we see money as a toy to play with instead of a tool to impact eternity, our vision becomes short-sighted and unfocused. As a result, our financial decisions and lifestyles become equally shortsighted and unfocused. Instead of acting like God's money managers, we live foolishly and wastefully, taking our cues not from the Owner, but from the world around us, which neither knows nor cares about what God wants us to do with his money. We need to learn to think and live differently. As Martin Luther put it, "There are three conversions necessary in the Christian life: the conversion of the heart, the mind, and the purse."

We were made for a person and a place. Jesus is the person and Heaven is the place. Letting this eternal perspective pervade our lives—including our view of what it means to be God's money managers—will unlock the door to exhilarating Christian discipleship, where "following Christ" is not a comforting yet meaningless cliché but an electrifying, life-changing reality.

Money and Possessions: Bible 101

CHAPTER 1

Starting Right:
A Biblical Mind-Set
about Money

Are we faithful in how we handle money?

First, we should come to grips with reality—even when we imagine we have little money, we have far more than we realize. Many who say, "I have nothing to give," spend large amounts of discretionary income on cars, clothes, coffee, entertainment, phones, computers, and so on. *They have nothing to give when they're done spending, precisely because they're never done spending.* Then, when they run out of money, they think it's because they didn't have enough.

In Luke 16, Jesus suggests that all of us are continually tested in our money management: "If you are faithful in little things, you will be faithful in large ones. But if you are dishonest in little things, you won't be honest with greater responsibilities. And if you are untrustworthy about worldly wealth, who will trust you with the true riches of heaven?" (Luke 16:10-11).

This principle invalidates all of our "if onlys," such as "If only I made more money, I'd help the poor," or

"If only I had a million dollars, then I'd give it to my church or missions." If I'm dishonest or selfish in my use of a few dollars, I would be dishonest or selfish in my use of a million dollars. The issue is not what I would do with a million dollars if I had it, but what I *am* doing with the hundred thousand, ten thousand, or ten dollars I *do* have. If we are not faithful with what God has already entrusted to us, why should he trust us with any more?

Don't miss this: Jesus made a direct connection between our present handling of earthly wealth and his future decision to entrust to our care another kind of wealth. "If you are untrustworthy about worldly wealth, who will trust you with the true riches of heaven?" There is a direct connection between our faithful use of money here and now and the "true riches" God will put us over in his future Kingdom.

If a child can't be trusted to return the change after shopping with his father's money, neither can he be trusted to stay overnight at a friend's house. But if he's faithful to clean his room and do his chores, he can be trusted to have a bike or a dog.

God pays a great deal of attention to the "little things." He numbers the hairs on our heads, cares for the lilies of the field, and is concerned with the fall of a single sparrow (Luke 12:27-31; Matthew 10:29-30). As a business owner pays attention to how an employee handles the little things, God pays attention to us. What we do with a little time, a little talent, and a little money tells God a lot. The little things are a major factor as he considers whether to commend and promote us—or reprimand and demote us—in his Kingdom operation.

This thought raises a sobering question: What opportunities are we missing, or will we one day miss, because we've failed to use money wisely in light of eternity?

Is money really important to God?

Thousands of verses of Scripture talk directly or indirectly about money and possessions and how God's people should use them. The sheer enormity of the Bible's teaching on this subject screams for our attention. Why did Jesus say more about how we are to view and handle money and possessions than about any other topic—including both Heaven and Hell, and prayer and faith? Because God wants us to recognize the powerful relationship between our true spiritual condition and our attitude and actions concerning money and possessions.

Jesus' interaction with Zacchaeus gives us insight into what God thinks about money. "Zacchaeus stood before the Lord and said, 'I will give half my wealth to the poor, Lord, and if I have cheated people on their taxes, I will give them back four times as much!' Jesus responded, 'Salvation has come to this home today, for this man has shown himself to be a true son of Abraham'" (Luke 19:8-9).

Jesus judged the reality of Zacchaeus's salvation by

his willingness—his cheerful eagerness—to part with his money for God's glory and the good of others.

In contrast to Zacchaeus, Matthew 19:16-25 recounts the rich young ruler's dilemma:

Someone came to Jesus with this question: "Teacher, what good deed must I do to have eternal life?" . . . "If you want to receive eternal life, keep the commandments." "Which ones?" the man asked. And Jesus replied: "You must not murder. You must not commit adultery. You must not steal. You must not testify falsely. Honor your father and mother. Love your neighbor as yourself." "I've obeyed all these commandments," the young man replied. "What else must I do?" Jesus told him, "If you want to be perfect, go and sell all your possessions and give the money to the poor, and you will have treasure in heaven. Then come, follow me." But when the young man heard this, he went away sad, for he had many possessions. Then Jesus said to his disciples, "I tell you the truth, it is very hard for a rich person to enter the Kingdom of Heaven. I'll say it again—it is easier for a camel to go through the eye of a needle than for a rich person to enter the Kingdom of God!" The disciples were astounded.

In response to the rich young ruler, Jesus expounded the moral perfection of keeping all God's commandments. The man assured Jesus he had kept them. But Jesus tested him on the first and last commandments: "You must not have any other god but me" and "You must not covet."

After losing this potential follower, a man so sincere that he was grieved to turn away, Jesus astonished his disciples by telling them that it's very hard for rich people to enter the Kingdom of Heaven. They didn't understand the barrier that wealth presents to genuine spiritual birth and growth. *Apparently, neither do we.*

Jesus did not call each and every disciple to liquidate their possessions, give away all their money, and leave their homes. But Jesus knew that money was the rich young man's god. The principle is timeless: If Christ is not Lord over our money and possessions, he is not our Lord.

Why so much biblical emphasis on money and possessions?

In the following passage, though no one asks John the Baptist about money and possessions, notice carefully his answers to their questions:

> When the crowds came to John for baptism, he said, "You brood of snakes! Who warned you to flee God's coming wrath? Prove by the way you live that you have repented of your

sins and turned to God. . . . Even now the ax
of God's judgment is poised, ready to sever
the roots of the trees. Yes, every tree that does
not produce good fruit will be chopped down
and thrown into the fire." The crowds asked,
"What should we do?" John replied, "If you
have two shirts, give one to the poor. If you
have food, share it with those who are hungry."
Even corrupt tax collectors came to be
baptized and asked, "Teacher, what should we
do?" He replied, "Collect no more taxes than
the government requires." "What should we
do?" asked some soldiers. John replied, "Don't
extort money or make false accusations. And
be content with your pay." (Luke 3:7-14)

John's instructions *all* relate to money and possessions: Share clothes and food with the poor, don't take
more than what's due you, be content with your wages,
don't extort money or accuse falsely (this probably refers
to the practice of claiming that someone's possessions
were stolen goods so that soldiers could confiscate and
keep them). Those things were of such high priority, so
close to the heart of following God, that John couldn't
talk about true repentance and spiritual transformation
without addressing them.

Luke, the writer of Acts, offers dramatic accounts of
believers whose faith had a significant impact on their
pocketbooks: "Many who became believers confessed
their sinful practices. A number of them who had been

practicing sorcery brought their incantation books and burned them at a public bonfire. *The value of the books was several million dollars.* So the message about the Lord spread widely and had a powerful effect" (Acts 19:18-20[1]).

Nobody burns sorcery books worth millions of dollars unless they're convinced God is telling them to. It was no more natural for those first-century Christians to cheerfully liquidate and disburse assets they'd spent their lives accumulating than it would be for us. That's the whole point. Conversion and the filling of the Holy Spirit are *super*natural experiences that produce supernatural responses—whether in the first century or the twenty-first.

Suppose Luke or John the Baptist were to visit us today and gauge *our* spiritual condition by *our* attitudes and actions regarding money and possessions. What conclusions would they draw?

Isn't what we do with our money our own business?

In Mark 12:41-44, we see that our Lord notices—and cares—what people do with their money. "Jesus sat down near the collection box in the Temple and watched as the crowds dropped in their money. Many rich people put in large amounts. Then a poor widow came and dropped in two small coins. Jesus called his disciples to him and said, 'I tell you the truth, this poor

---

1 Italics in Scripture are mine throughout the book.

widow has given more than all the others who are making contributions. For they gave a tiny part of their surplus, but she, poor as she is, has given everything she had to live on.'"

Notice the passage doesn't say, "Jesus happened to see. . . ." No, Jesus deliberately *watched* what people were giving. Jesus was close enough to see two tiny coins in a shriveled old hand, and he was interested enough in what people were giving to make an object lesson for his disciples. God makes no apology for paying attention to what we do with the money he's entrusted to us—or for challenging us to raise the bar of our own giving by taking to heart the example of others' generosity.

A striking parable of Jesus further demonstrates that God sees what we do with our money and judges us accordingly:

A rich man had a fertile farm that produced fine crops. He said to himself, "What should I do? I don't have room for all my crops." Then he said, "I know! I'll tear down my barns and build bigger ones. Then I'll have room enough to store all my wheat and other goods. And I'll sit back and say to myself, 'My friend, you have enough stored away for years to come. Now take it easy! Eat, drink, and be merry!'" But God said to him, "You fool! You will die this very night. Then who will get everything you worked for?" Yes, a person is a fool to store up earthly wealth but not have a rich relationship with God. Then, turning to his disciples, Jesus said, "That is why I tell you not to worry about everyday life—whether you have enough food to eat or enough clothes to wear." (Luke 12:16-22)

The rich fool of Luke 12 stands in stark contrast to the poor widow of Mark 12. He may have attended synagogue weekly, visited the Temple three times a year, tithed, and prayed, as most Jews did. Now, like any good businessman, he wanted to expand by building bigger barns. His purpose was to accumulate enough wealth to retire early and have a good time. Sounds just like the American dream, doesn't it?

Take careful notice: *The God who knows hearts and sees from the vantage point of eternity regards the poor woman as eternally wise and the rich man as eternally foolish.* Why? Because one was rich toward God and the other wasn't. Yet who do most Western Christians think and live more like—the poor widow or the rich fool?

Let's be honest—if asked, wouldn't many of us congratulate the rich fool for his entrepreneurial enterprise and warn the poor woman to hold on to what little money she had? Our beliefs about money are often diametrically opposed to God's. This is why we should thoughtfully and prayerfully meditate on what Scripture tells us.

What questions will we one day have to answer?
Studying Zacchaeus, the rich young ruler, the poor widow, and other Bible characters reveals that how we handle money is an accurate index of our spiritual lives. This is true of all people in all ages. But it's particularly true for most readers of this book, since we live in a place and time when what our government calls the "poverty level" far exceeds the average standard of living of nearly every other society in human history, past and present.

According to Romans 14:12, "Each of us will give a personal account to God." One day we will all have to answer these and other questions: What did I do with all that wealth? What has my handling of money and possessions accomplished for eternity?

CHAPTER 2

Ownership:
It All Belongs to God

A DISTRAUGHT MAN frantically rode his horse up to John Wesley, shouting, "Mr. Wesley, Mr. Wesley, something terrible has happened! Your house has burned to the ground!"

Weighing the news for the moment, Wesley replied, "No. The Lord's house burned to the ground. That means one less responsibility for me."

We might say, "Get real," but Wesley's reaction didn't stem from a denial of reality. Rather, it sprang from life's most basic reality—that God is the owner of all things, and we are simply his stewards.

Jerry Caven had a successful restaurant chain, two banks, a ranch, a farm, and several real estate ventures. At age fifty-nine, he was searching for a nice lakeside retirement home. But the Owner had other plans.

"God led us to put our money and time overseas," Jerry says. "It's been exciting. Before, we gave token amounts. Now we put substantial money into missions. We often go to India."

What changed the Cavens's attitude toward giving?

"It was realizing God's ownership," Jerry explains. "Once we understood we were giving away God's money to do God's work, we discovered a peace and joy we never had back when we thought it was our money!"

John Wesley and Jerry Caven have something in common that all of us need to cultivate: a life-changing understanding of God's ownership and our stewardship.

What is stewardship, and why is ownership foundational to it?

Back in 1988, while writing the first version of my book *Money, Possessions, and Eternity*, I was tempted not to use the word *stewardship*. It seemed an old and dying word that conjured up images of large red thermometers on church platforms, measuring how far the churches were from paying off the mortgage.

Still, I decided that stewardship was just too good a word, both biblically and historically, to abandon. I'm glad I didn't abandon the word, because in recent years it has gained new traction. Not only Christians but also unbelievers frequently talk about "stewardship of the earth" and "stewardship of the environment."

The foundational meaning of stewardship is found not in secular culture but in its biblical roots. We'll explore in the next chapter what Jesus taught in his stewardship parables. But for now, we can simply define a steward as "*someone an owner entrusts with the management of his assets.*"

There can be no understanding of stewardship until there is an accute awareness of *ownership*. The steward cannot do his job well without clearly grasping who owns—and who does *not* own—what is entrusted to his care.

Is God really the owner of all?

From beginning to end, Scripture emphasizes God's ownership of everything. Consider carefully the cumulative weight of these verses:

- "The earth is the LORD's, and everything in it, the world, and all who live in it" (Psalm 24:1, NIV).
- "To the LORD your God belong the heavens, even the highest heavens, the earth and everything in it" (Deuteronomy 10:14, NIV).
- "The land is mine and you are but aliens and my tenants" (Leviticus 25:23, NIV).
- "Yours, O LORD, is the greatness and the power and the glory and the majesty and the splendor, for everything in heaven and earth is yours. Yours, O LORD, is the kingdom; you are exalted as head over all. Wealth and honor come from you; you are the ruler of all things" (1 Chronicles 29:11-12, NIV).
- "Who has a claim against me that I must pay? Everything under heaven belongs to me" (Job 41:11, NIV).

- "For every animal of the forest is mine, and the cattle on a thousand hills. I know every bird in the mountains, and the creatures of the field are mine. If I were hungry I would not tell you, for the world is mine, and all that is in it" (Psalm 50:10-12, NIV).
- "'The silver is mine and the gold is mine,' declares the LORD Almighty" (Haggai 2:8, NIV).

It's hard to imagine a more comprehensive declaration of absolute divine ownership of everything. Furthermore, search carefully, and you won't find a single verse of Scripture that suggests God has ever surrendered his ownership to us!

And if we should think, *Well, at least I own myself,* God says, "You are not your own; you were bought at a price" (1 Corinthians 6:19-20, NIV).

God doesn't own just the universe; he owns you and me. If we're his children, we are twice his—first by creation, second by redemption.

Stewardship includes the divinely delegated management of our physical, mental, and spiritual lives, and the exercise of our God-given gifts and skills. Our stewardship encompasses the protection of human life—caring for the young, disabled, vulnerable, and oppressed. We are stewards of our families, workplaces, communities, churches, and nations. We're caretakers of animals and the earth's environment. God has entrusted all these to us. But worthy as those causes are, *Managing God's Money* is not about stewardship in general but about financial stewardship in particular. That itself gives us plenty to talk about.

Not only does God own everything, but he grants us our money-making skills and determines how much of his wealth he will entrust to us:

- "Remember the LORD your God, for it is he who gives you the ability to produce wealth" (Deuteronomy 8:18, NIV).
- "The LORD makes poor and makes rich; He brings low and lifts up" (1 Samuel 2:7, NKJV).

In the financial world, a good investment manager doesn't do with his client's holdings what he feels like. Why? Because he knows *those assets don't belong to him*; they belong to his client. Good stewards always act in the owners' best interests, consulting and listening carefully to the owner in order to understand and implement his investment priorities.

Read, reread, and memorize the "God is the owner" passages cited at the beginning of this section. Stewardship—properly serving as God's asset managers—requires constantly living in light of God's ownership.

John Wesley, who affirmed it was God's house that had burned down, posed four questions to help us decide how to spend money. Notice how the last three flow directly out of the first one:

- In spending this money, am I acting as if I owned it, or am I acting as the Lord's trustee?
- What Scripture passage requires me to spend this money in this way?
- Can I offer up this purchase as a sacrifice to the Lord?
- Will God reward me for this expenditure at the resurrection of the just?

If we really believe God is the owner of all that has been entrusted to us, shouldn't we be regularly asking him, "What do you want me to do with *your* money and *your* possessions?" And shouldn't we be open to the possibility that he may want us to share large portions of his assets with those whose needs are greater than ours?

How is stewardship synonymous with the Christian life?

God expects us to use all the resources he gives us to best carry out our responsibilities in furthering his Kingdom. This includes caring for our families, our homes and businesses, our planet, and whatever else he entrusts to us.

A steward's primary goal is to be "found faithful" by his master. He proves himself faithful by wisely using the master's resources to accomplish the tasks delegated to him (1 Corinthians 4:2). Those resources include not only money but time, gifting, relationships, employment, and life opportunities.

Seen from this perspective, stewardship isn't a narrow subcategory of the Christian life. On the contrary, stewardship *is* the Christian life. God's ownership of not only "our" money and possessions but "our" time and abilities and everything else should be central in our thinking.

When teaching from 1 Corinthians 6—"You are not your own; you were bought at a price" (NIV)— I occasionally ask someone in the front row to lend me her pencil. When she hands it to me, I break it in half, throw it on the floor, and crush it under my foot. The reaction of the students is shock and disbelief. What right do I have to break someone else's pencil? When I explain that it's really *my* pencil, which I planted before the session, everything changes. If it belongs to me, I have the right to do with it what I want.

Many of our problems begin when we forget that God is the boss of the universe. But in fact he is more than the boss; he is the *owner*. I might resent a powerful person for taking control, but everything changes if I realize he owns everything, and therefore, *he has the right to do what he chooses.*

As long as I hold tightly to something, I believe I own it. But when I give it away, I relinquish control, power, and prestige. When I realize that God has a claim not merely on the few dollars I might choose to throw in an offering plate, not simply on 10 percent or even 50 percent, but on 100 percent of "my" money, it's revolutionary. If I'm God's money manager, I'm not God. Money isn't God. *God* is God. So God, money, and I are each put in our rightful place.

Not only does God own everything; God controls everything. The implications are enormous. I can resign my self-appointed role as god. I don't have to try to control everything (which never worked well, come to think of it). The universe is in better hands than mine. And even what God has placed in my hands remains his, not mine.

God's ownership and sovereignty offer a life-changing and freeing perspective when the house is robbed (or burns to the ground), the car is totaled, the laptop computer is stolen . . . or the diagnosis is terminal cancer.

When we come to Christ, God puts all his resources at our disposal. He also expects us to put all our resources at *his* disposal. This is what stewardship is all about.

If we believe God is the owner of all that has been entrusted to us, we see that what we do as his employees puts his assets and his reputation on the line. It is then that we discover the question we should have been asking him all along: What do you want me to do with *your* money and *your* possessions?

CHAPTER 3

Stewardship: It's under Our Management

IN THIS CHAPTER we'll explore the stewardship parables of Jesus by taking a close look at one and then summarizing the central teachings of all.

Christ's parable of the shrewd manager, sometimes called the "unrighteous steward," concerns a wealthy owner who fires his business manager for wasting his assets (Luke 16:1-13). During the brief period before his termination becomes effective, the steward goes to his master's debtors and reduces what they owe, thereby engendering their friendship. When the master learns of this, he doesn't praise the steward for unethical behavior—but he *does* praise him for his foresight in making friends who will be supportive of him now that his term of stewardship is over.

The man's termination signifies that every steward's service will one day come to an end. We will finish this life just as the manager finished his job, and likely just as unexpectedly. When that time comes, we, too, will give an account of our stewardship (Romans 14:12).

Consequently, Jesus is telling us, we should follow the steward's example of looking ahead to the long-term future and using wisely what little remaining time and influence we have now.

What are the eternal friends and dwellings Jesus speaks of?

In this parable, Jesus doesn't tell us to stay away from "worldly wealth" but to use it strategically. He says to use it "to gain friends for yourselves, so that when it is gone, you will be welcomed into eternal dwellings" (Luke 16:9, NIV).

Money can be a tool of Christ. But it must be used as such now, before our current period of service ends. There will be no second chance to use our present money for Christ in the next life. After the manager's termination was effective, after he could work no longer, the manager would have no more leverage. He used his final days of service to win friends who could take him into their dwellings when his work was done.

Jesus tells us that after we die, we may be welcomed by friends into eternal dwellings. Perhaps the friends of this parable will participate in the "rich welcome" upon entering Heaven (2 Peter 1:11, NIV). Their participation in that welcoming will be contingent upon our wise use of our God-entrusted resources on Earth to impact these "friends."

But who are these friends? They're believers who are in Heaven as a result of our ministry or whose lives we've touched in a significant way through the use of our material assets. Apparently, they'll have their own "eternal dwellings" and will welcome us in so that we may have a place to stay as we move about the heavenly Kingdom. What a wonderful thought! This is encouraging in light of redeemed family members, friends, and others we've influenced, and for the many we don't even know yet who've been touched by our prayers, service, and financial giving.

This idea is very strange to many Christians, but it shouldn't be. That believers will have their own living quarters in Heaven is substantiated by other texts. The New Jerusalem is a physical place (Revelation 21:16). To qualify as a "city," it presumably consists of individual residences (Revelation 21:2). Jesus says that he is preparing eternal dwelling places for us (John 14:2-3).

He tells us we will eat and drink at tables together (Matthew 8:11; Revelation 19:9). Given the physical nature of our resurrection bodies, why should we be surprised to find that we will be able to welcome each other into our homes?

The Carpenter from Galilee is constructing residences for us. (His previous experience creating a universe should come in handy!) If we integrate a similar analogy, 1 Corinthians 3:10-15 suggests that in this life we're providing the building materials for our Lord to use in this construction project, of which he himself is the foundation. Perhaps the size and quality of our eternal dwelling may be influenced by how faithfully we manage God's assets now. This certainly fits with the concept of reward being commensurate to service, as taught in 2 Corinthians 5:10 and in all the stewardship parables.

As God's asset managers, what kind of building materials are we sending ahead? Whom have we influenced spiritually to the point that they would welcome us into their eternal dwelling places? To which needy people have we sacrificially given our resources to the glory of God?

Every time we give to world missions, famine relief, prison ministry, and Bible translation, whenever we invest our time and prayers, we can dream about the day we'll meet and enjoy the hospitality of new friends and family, precious people in Heaven.

One day, money will be useless. While it's still useful, God's money managers with foresight will use it for eternal good.

What are the "true riches" Jesus entrusts to some?

Jesus elaborates on the story of the shrewd steward by saying, "If you have not been trustworthy in handling worldly wealth, who will trust you with true riches?" (Luke 16:11, NIV). What are "true riches"? Riches that God values, that will last for eternity. What could those be but other human beings with eternal souls? God tests us in the handling of money and possessions to determine the extent of our trustworthiness in dealing with people.

Having been faithful in handling our resources in this life, we will be granted leadership of others in the next (Luke 19:17, 19). Not only on the New Earth, where we will reign with Christ, but here and now, as we prove ourselves ready by managing well his material assets, God graciously entrusts to our care and influence greater riches—human beings created in his image.

How many Christians have forfeited eternally significant ministry to eternal souls because they have failed to handle their money well? Through mismanagement of God's estate, we can lose credibility with people as well as forfeit God's willingness to entrust us with more people to influence.

What do Christ's stewardship parables mean?

The story of the shrewd manager in Luke 16 is one of several stewardship parables. It shows that each of us should carefully invest our financial assets, gifts, and opportunities to have an impact on people for eternity, thereby making preparations for our own eternal future.

The parable of the talents (Matthew 25:14-30) shows that we're each entrusted by God with different financial assets, gifts, and opportunities, and we'll be held accountable to him for how we've invested them in this life. We're to prepare for the Master's return by enhancing the growth of his Kingdom through wisely investing his assets.

The parable of the ten minas (Luke 19:11-27)

shows that those with comparable gifts, assets, and opportunities will be judged according to their faithfulness, industriousness, and wisdom while investing in God's Kingdom. Consequently, in God's eternal Kingdom, they'll receive varying positions of authority, which Jesus describes as ruling over cities, apparently on the New Earth.

What does Jesus teach us about the property owner?

Each of the stewardship parables has two major subjects: the master and the servants. First, I'll summarize the lessons concerning the master:

Ownership. The master is the true owner of all assets. The possessions, the money—even the servants—belong to the master. He has the right to do with everything as he wishes.

Authority. The master's will is final; his decisions are determinative.

Trust. The master has delegated to his servants significant financial assets and authority over his money and possessions. This indicates a level of trust in their ability to manage them. It also shows a willingness to risk delegating responsibilities to people who can and sometimes do fail.

Generosity. Although the master has the right to expect the servants to do what he commands without rewarding them, the owner graciously promises reward and promotion to his stewards who prove themselves faithful.

Expectations. The master has specific expectations of his stewards. They're not easy, but they're fair. He has every right to expect his stewards to do what he has told them to do. The servants know of his high standards and should not presume upon his grace by being lazy and disobedient. The master will take away whatever reward he would have given the servant who was unfaithful and will discipline him for poor stewardship. Meanwhile, he will delight in pouring out reward upon his faithful servants.

What does Jesus teach us about the property manager?

Stewardship. The servants should be acutely aware that they are only caretakers or money managers. It's their job to take the assets entrusted (not given) to them and use them wisely to care for and expand the master's estate.

Accountability. Because they don't own these assets, the servants are accountable for them to the master. They will stand before him one day to explain why they invested as they did.

One servant's efforts will not be sullied by the incompetence of others. The master may deal with other servants however he wishes. Each servant must do the job assigned to him and be prepared to give account to one from whom nothing can be hidden (Hebrews 4:13).

Faithfulness. Servants seek to be trustworthy, to handle their master's estate in a way that would please him. They do this until the master returns or until death, no matter how many years it may be until then. Stewardship is the servant's life calling. Resignation isn't an option.

Industriousness. The servants must work hard and do their best.

Wisdom. Because they are managing the master's assets, servants must choose their investments carefully. They can neither afford to take undue risks nor let capital erode through idleness. The goal isn't merely to conserve resources but to multiply them. The servants must be wise, resourceful, and strategic thinkers regarding the best long-term investments.

Respect. The stewards know that the master is just. His instructions are explicit and his expectations high. The master's generosity ensures that the stewards will be handsomely rewarded if they work wisely. But they also know that if they're unfaithful, they will feel the master's wrath. This healthy fear motivates them to good stewardship.

Focus. All side interests are brought into orbit around the steward's one consuming purpose in life— to serve the master well.

In a context that leads to the statement that "each of us will give an account of himself to God," Paul asks,

"Who are you to judge someone else's servant? To his own master he stands or falls" (Romans 14:4, 12, NIV).

When we stand before our Master and Maker, it will not matter how many people on Earth knew our names, how many called us great, or how many considered us fools. It will not matter whether schools and hospitals were named after us, whether our estates were large or small, whether our funerals drew ten thousand or no one. What will matter is one thing and one thing only—what our Master thinks of us.

Are we ready for the Owner to return or for us to go to him?

A man went to visit the caretaker of a large estate with an absentee owner. Noticing how meticulously the caretaker performed every chore, the visitor asked him, "When do you expect the owner to return?" The caretaker's reply: "Today, of course."

Like soldiers ready at any moment for a barracks inspection, servants are constantly aware that this could be the day of the master's return. If they knew the day or hour of that return, they could waste time. They might "borrow" some of the master's money, intending to replace it before he comes back. When they cease to expect the master's return, embezzlement or squandering becomes a great temptation. But if the stewards know that the master is a man of his word, they live each day as if it were the day of the master's return. Because one day it will be.

Either Christ's second coming or our deaths bring us to stand before our Lord. Either event marks the end of our current service as his asset managers. At that moment, our service record irrevocably "freezes" into its final form, to be evaluated as such by our Master at the judgment.

The apostle Paul warns us against complacency: "You know quite well that the day of the Lord's return will come unexpectedly, like a thief in the night. When people are saying, 'Everything is peaceful and secure,' then disaster will fall on them as suddenly as a pregnant woman's labor pains begin. And there will be no escape. But you aren't in the dark about these things, dear brothers and sisters, and you won't be surprised when the day of the Lord comes like a thief" (1 Thessalonians 5:2-4).

The thief's design is to make his victims poorer by taking their treasures. If our treasures are on Earth, Christ's return will indeed make us poorer, because it will take away our earthly treasures just as surely as a thief raiding a house.

But if we've stored up our treasures in Heaven, Christ's return will not *take* treasures *from* us, but *bring* treasures *to* us. Christ will turn the thief analogy on its head, because the faithful believer will not become poorer when Christ returns, but immeasurably richer!

Even if Christ does not return for two hundred years, we will meet him in our deaths, whether in twenty years, twenty months, or twenty minutes. God encourages us not to be surprised about the soon coming of our appointment to stand before him. If we are ready to meet Christ, we will long for his return. If we are not ready, we will dread it. If we do not feel ready to meet him, now is the time to get ready.

As God's child and his money manager, what personal, spiritual, moral, and financial changes do you need to make to get ready to give him a face-to-face account of your job performance?

Perspectives That Impede Faithful Money Management

CHAPTER 4

"Money Is Bad": A False Spirituality

HAVING EXAMINED THE Bible's emphasis on God's ownership and our stewardship, you may be struggling with how countercultural these concepts are, both in the world and in the church. To go deeper in our understanding of how we can serve as God's faithful money managers, we need to expose the deeply entrenched false perspectives that argue against what God tells us in his Word and hinder us from thinking correctly and living obediently. The next five chapters are dedicated to this end.

If we fail to see how radically different these contrasting worldviews are, we will make the critical error of understanding God's Word in light of our culture, thereby stripping it of its meaning and power. It is vital that we reverse this process. In these chapters we will seek to understand our culture in light of God's Word, freeing us to embrace not what is currently popular in either the world or church cultures but what the Bible actually tells us.

Does the Bible say money is evil?

Two equally incorrect beliefs about money are that it is always evil and that it is always good.

But doesn't the Bible say that "money is the root of all evil"? No, it does not. What it says is this: "The *love of money* is the root of all kinds of evil" (1 Timothy 6:10).

Men have betrayed their countries for financial gain. This is evil, but the evil doesn't reside in the money. It resides in the men. Money isn't evil; money love is evil.

First Timothy 4:4-5 says, "Since everything God created is good, we should not reject any of it but receive it with thanks. For we know it is made acceptable by the word of God and prayer."

Money can be used to buy a slave or a whip to be used on a slave. Money can purchase sex, bribe a judge, buy cocaine, and fund terrorist acts. In each case, the people using the money are evil, but money itself is not evil. Likewise, when a woman gives her money to help the poor, it isn't the money that's good; she is good. We should not scorn money but thank God for it, rejoicing that we can use it for honorable purposes. We should manage it wisely and use it thoughtfully and generously for God's glory and people's good.

God not only commanded his people Israel to give, but he also told them they could convert their material assets to money. Then they could use it to buy food to celebrate with their families in a feast to be enjoyed in God's presence (Deuteronomy 14:24-26). In other words, money could be used for God-honoring purposes.

Money merely symbolizes wealth. Gold, silver, platinum, coins, and currency are worth something only in a society where other people have agreed to attach value to them. Money is nothing more than a pledge of assets, a means of payment, a medium of exchange. People may be moral or immoral, but *things* are morally neutral and can be used for good purposes or bad.

Is it possible to both follow God *and* make money?

To regard money as evil, and therefore useless for purposes of righteousness, is foolish. To regard it as good, and therefore overlook its potential for spiritual disaster, is equally foolish. Jesus said, "No one can serve two masters. . . . You cannot serve both God and money" (Luke 16:13). Use money, but don't serve it. See it for what it is and for what it isn't. Money makes a terrible master, yet it makes a good servant to those who have the right master—God.

The goal, then, is not to put money to death, but to handle it with respect and discipline, like a lion we are seeking to tame.

Materialism is money centered and thing centered rather than God centered. As we'll see in subsequent chapters, it has no place in the Christian life. The other extreme is *asceticism*. Asceticism sees money and things as evil. To the ascetic, the less you own, the more spiritual you are. If something isn't essential, you shouldn't have it. Materialism and asceticism are rooted in equally wrong views of money and possessions.

Martin Luther compared humanity to a drunkard who falls off his horse to the right, gets back on, and then falls off to the left. Asceticism is falling off the horse on one side; materialism is falling off the other side. As Luther said, Satan doesn't care which side of the horse we fall off, as long as we don't stay in the saddle. Scripture portrays the relationship between the material and the spiritual not as either/or but as both/and. The material must not take precedence over the spiritual, but it is nonetheless a necessary and legitimate part of our existence.

Paul captured this principle when he thanked the Philippian church for supporting his ministry: "Not that I was ever in need, for I have learned how to be content with whatever I have. I know how to live on almost nothing or with everything. I have learned the secret of living in every situation, whether it is with a full stomach or empty, with plenty or little" (Philippians 4:11-12).

A proverb makes a similar point: "Give me neither poverty nor riches! Give me just enough to satisfy my needs. For if I grow rich, I may deny you and say, 'Who is the LORD?' And if I am too poor, I may steal and thus insult God's holy name" (Proverbs 30:8-9).

Our greatest resources are spiritual, not material. They come from another world, not this one. Paul had to *learn* contentment—that means it didn't come naturally for him. Contentment isn't the product of material abundance; it comes from accessing our intangible but very real resources in Christ.

Is it right for Christians to have material possessions and enjoy them?

The entire fabric of Old Testament teaching and Hebrew thought argues against platonic dualism (the theory that the body is bad and the soul is good; therefore, you can separate the two) and asceticism (the idea that anything physical, like money and possessions, is evil).

There are not two gods, a god of the spiritual and a god of the physical. The same God created both the spiritual and physical worlds for us to enjoy.

God's people Israel viewed material things as gifts from God's hand, as a Father's loving provision for his children. As his grateful children, they celebrated the harvest and national feasts, mandated in his law to them, to recognize and rejoice in his material provision. "For seven days you must celebrate this festival to honor the LORD your God at the place he chooses, for it is he who blesses you with bountiful harvests and gives you success in all your work. This festival will be a time of great joy for all" (Deuteronomy 16:15).

Generating income is a necessary and God-ordained part of life in the present world and is therefore not unspiritual. We should commend those who choose to live simply or strategically so that a larger portion of their income helps the needy. But we should neither disdain income production nor withdraw from "the system," as if economics were sinful. If we do, we'll end up contributing to poverty rather than alleviating it. We must all battle materialism—not by withdrawing from society, but by serving God faithfully within it.

CHAPTER 5

"It's All about Money": The False God of Materialism

What's wrong with wanting things?

God created us to love people and use things, but materialists love things and use people. Products are marketed to "consumers" without regard for the fact that they may become addicted, depressed, obese, or diseased—taking years off their lives—as a result of consuming those products. Materialism drives not just the "bad apples" of society; it drives "the best and the brightest," those from the finest homes and schools, those who become government and business leaders, physicians, and attorneys.

God, of course, knows our tendency to take advantage of others when it comes to money. In his law, he told his people, "When you make an agreement with your neighbor to buy or sell property, you must not take advantage of each other" (Leviticus 25:14). But the people didn't listen. Centuries later God's prophet proclaimed, "The LORD comes forward to pronounce judgment on the elders and rulers of his people: 'You have ruined Israel, my vineyard. Your houses are filled with things stolen from the poor'" (Isaiah 3:14).

The same is true everywhere. Materialism is cross-cultural and pan-ethnic. It was true of some religious leaders in Jesus' day, and of some in our own: "They shamelessly cheat widows out of their property and then pretend to be pious by making long prayers in public. Because of this, they will be more severely punished" (Mark 12:40).

Materialists simply live out what they've learned at home, at school, from the media, from their friends—and sometimes, sadly, even from their churches. A materialistic world can never be won to Christ by a materialistic church. Paul recommended an alternative: "Don't just pretend to love others. Really love them. Hate what is wrong. Hold tightly to what is good" (Romans 12:9).

Bible stories too close to home?

Materialism's sad stories fill the pages of Scripture.

When the walls of Jericho fell, Achan stole things set apart for God and thought he could get away with it. He didn't (Joshua 7:1-26).

For a fee, Delilah betrayed Samson to the Philistines (Judges 16:4-8).

To gain wealth, Gehazi lied about Elisha's desire to receive payment for curing Naaman (2 Kings 5:20-27). For this act of greed, God afflicted Gehazi with the leprosy he cured Naaman of.

Long before the Israelites had their first king, God warned against a monarch's temptation to materialism: "The king must not build up a large stable of horses for himself or send his people to Egypt to buy horses, for the LORD has told you, 'You must never return to Egypt.' The king must not take many wives for himself, because they will turn his heart away from the LORD. And he must not accumulate large amounts of wealth in silver and gold for himself" (Deuteronomy 17:16-17).

Unfortunately, Solomon's lust for more and more wealth led him to flagrantly disobey God's prohibitions against amassing large quantities of horses, gold, silver, and wives. And, just as God had warned, Solomon's heart turned away from him.

In the ultimate act of treachery, Judas betrayed God's Son for money. "Judas Iscariot, one of the twelve disciples, went to the leading priests and asked, 'How much will you pay me to betray Jesus to you?' And they gave him thirty pieces of silver. From that time on, Judas began looking for an opportunity to betray Jesus" (Matthew 26:14-16).

What *isn't* life measured by?

Jesus Christ sounded a sober warning against materialism in any form and in any age: "Watch out! Be on your guard against all kinds of greed; a man's life does not consist in the abundance of his possessions" (Luke 12:15, NIV).

Paul saw greed as a serious sin, lumping it together with sexual immorality and equating it with idolatry: "Put to death the sinful, earthly things lurking within you. Have nothing to do with sexual immorality, impurity, lust, and evil desires. Don't be greedy, for a greedy person is an idolater, worshiping the things of this world" (Colossians 3:5).

Greed surfaces in possessiveness and covetousness. Possessiveness relates to what we have, being selfish with what we own, not quick to share. Covetousness relates to what we want—longing for and being preoccupied with having what God hasn't given us, having a passion to possess what is not ours.

It takes time to hover over our things, and that time must come from elsewhere—time we might spend cultivating intimacy with God, time in his Word and in prayer, time with family, time visiting the needy, time with people who need Christ. Every item I add to my possessions is one more thing to think about, talk about, clean, repair, display, rearrange, and replace when it goes bad. Acquiring a possession may also push me into redefining my priorities, making me unavailable for ministry. If I buy a boat, the problem isn't just the money. I must now justify my purchase by *using* the boat, which may mean frequent weekends away from church, making me unavailable to teach a Sunday school class, or work in the nursery, or lead a small group, or . . . fill in the blank. (Obviously, I'm not just talking about boats—substitute the material possessions you value most.)

As Jesus said, worries and wealth can choke us, making us unfruitful: "Now listen to the explanation of the parable about the farmer planting seeds: . . . The seed that fell among the thorns represents those who hear God's word, but all too quickly the message is crowded out by the worries of this life and the lure of wealth, so no fruit is produced. The seed that fell on good soil represents those who truly hear and understand God's word and produce a harvest of thirty, sixty, or even a hundred times as much as had been planted!" (Matthew 13:18, 22-23).

Is money-love a formula for self-destruction?

"People who long to be rich fall into temptation and are trapped by many foolish and harmful desires that plunge them into ruin and destruction. . . . And some people, craving money, have wandered from the true faith and pierced themselves with many sorrows" (1 Timothy 6:9-10).

Seeking fulfillment in money, land, houses, cars, clothes, RVs, hot tubs, large-screen televisions, luxury vacations, and cruises has left us bound and gagged by materialism—and like addicts, we think our only hope lies in getting more of the same. Meanwhile, the voice of God—unheard amid the clamor of our possessions—is telling us that even if materialism did bring happiness in this life (which it certainly does not), it would leave us woefully unprepared for the next life.

If we maintained God's perspective, even for a

moment, and saw how we go through life accumulating, hoarding, displaying, and serving our things, we would have the same feelings of horror and pity that any sane person has when viewing asylum inmates endlessly beating their heads against the wall.

CHAPTER 6

Materialism:
Ten Fatal Dangers

BEYOND THE EXAMPLES in Scripture of many people who are warped and destroyed by greed, and its warnings against idolatry, the Bible also lists various dangers of becoming centered on money and possessions. Warning: Don't dismiss this as negativism. On the contrary, if we understand the dangers of materialism, it will help liberate us to experience the joys of Christ-centered stewardship.

(1) Materialism hinders or destroys our spiritual lives

Jesus rebuked the Laodicean Christians because, although they were materially wealthy, they were desperately poor in the things of God. "You say, 'I am rich. I have everything I want. I don't need a thing!' And you don't realize that you are wretched and miserable and poor and blind and naked" (Revelation 3:17).

Materialism blinds us to our spiritual poverty. It's a

fruitless attempt to find meaning outside of God, the Source of all life and the giver of all good gifts.

(2) Materialism is a broken cistern that can't hold water

The prophet Jeremiah pointed out materialism's detrimental effect on a nation: "'Has any nation ever traded its gods for new ones, even though they are not gods at all? Yet my people have exchanged their glorious God for worthless idols! The heavens are shocked at such a thing and shrink back in horror and dismay,' says the LORD. 'For my people have done two evil things: They have abandoned me—the fountain of living water. And they have dug for themselves cracked cisterns that can hold no water at all!'" (Jeremiah 2:11-13).

A life centered on money and possessions is not only misguided; it's utterly self-destructive. It's not only wrong; it's stupid. In stark contrast, the Christ-centered life is not only right; it's smart. It sometimes pays off in the short run, and it *always* pays off in the long run.

(3) Materialism blinds us to the curses of wealth

As the Israelites traveled into the desert after their miraculous Exodus from Egypt, God provided manna, but the people weren't satisfied, so they *demanded* meat. God sent them meat in abundance, so much that it became a curse rather than a blessing (Numbers 11:18-20).

One of life's greatest ironies is the change that occurs

when a poor and humble person who walks with God is rewarded with prosperity. Often the person's attention gradually turns away from the Lord. Unless corrected, she will ultimately be transformed into a proud, rich person who comes under God's judgment. Ezekiel said to the king of Tyre, "With your wisdom and understanding you have amassed great wealth—gold and silver for your treasuries. Yes, your wisdom has made you very rich, and your riches have made you very proud" (Ezekiel 28:4-5).

Some wonder why God still blesses with wealth many once-godly Western nations. Perhaps the "blessing" is but a curse in disguise. In contrast, times of financial struggle may be God's character-building gift to us. In the midst of prosperity, the challenge for believers is to handle wealth so that it acts as a blessing, not a curse.

John Steinbeck wrote a letter to Adlai Stevenson, which was recorded in the January 28, 1960, edition of the *Washington Post*. Steinbeck said, "If I wanted to destroy a nation, I would give it too much, and I would have it on its knees, miserable, greedy, sick."

(4) Materialism brings us unhappiness and anxiety

The bait of wealth hides the hook of addiction and slavery. No wonder Christ's statement about not storing up treasures on Earth but in Heaven is immediately followed by this admonition: "So don't worry about these things, saying, 'What will we eat? What will we drink? What will we wear?' These things dominate the thoughts of unbelievers, but your heavenly Father already knows all your needs. Seek the Kingdom of God above all else, and live righteously, and he will give you everything you need. So don't worry about tomorrow, for tomorrow will bring its own worries. Today's trouble is enough for today" (Matthew 6:31-34).

People store up treasures on Earth rather than in Heaven, not only because of greed and selfishness, but also because of fear and insecurity. Yet putting our hope in earthly treasures does nothing but multiply anxiety. Why? Because earthly treasures are so temporary and uncertain. They cannot bear the weight of our trust. Solomon captured a profound truth: "The sleep of a laborer is sweet, whether he eats little or much, but the abundance of a rich man permits him no sleep" (Ecclesiastes 5:12, NIV).

A stockholder's hopes will rise and fall with the market. If what you treasure most is deposited in the bank and the bank fails, your heart will fail with it. In contrast, one who hopes in God will be devastated only if God fails—and he never does.

(5) Materialism ends in futility

The book of Ecclesiastes is the most powerful exposé of materialism ever written. In it, Solomon, one of history's wealthiest men, recounts his attempts to find meaning in building projects, entertainment, alcohol, sex, and possessions. "I said to myself, 'Come on, let's try pleasure. Let's look for the "good things" in life.' But I found that this, too, was meaningless. . . . I collected great sums of silver and gold, the treasure of many kings and provinces. . . . I had everything a man could desire! . . . Anything I wanted, I would take. I denied myself no pleasure" (Ecclesiastes 2:1, 8-10).

After decades as the world's richest man, Solomon said, "But as I looked at everything I had worked so hard to accomplish, it was all so meaningless—like chasing the wind. There was nothing really worthwhile anywhere" (Ecclesiastes 2:11).

Since the money god never keeps its promises, the more wealth Solomon accumulated, the more empty and meaningless his life became. "Those who love money will never have enough. How meaningless to think that wealth brings true happiness! The more you have, the more people come to help you spend it. So what good is wealth—except perhaps to watch it slip through your fingers!" (Ecclesiastes 5:10-11).

In contrast to materialism's emptiness, there is joyful liberty in Christ. Those who hold tightly to the true God will loosen their grip on money—and thereby loosen money's grip on them. Paul wrote, "Our hearts ache, but we always have joy. We are poor, but we give spiritual riches to others. We own nothing, and yet we have everything" (2 Corinthians 6:10).

(6) Materialism obscures many of life's greatest blessings

Ironically, those blessings are often far more appreciated by the poor, whose lives are less cluttered and distracted by material wealth. God's greatest gift of salvation is available to all and cannot be bought with money: "Is anyone thirsty? Come and drink—even if you have no money! Come, take your choice of wine or milk—it's all free!" (Isaiah 55:1).

God's Son redeemed us, freely giving himself to all who seek him. "The Spirit and the bride say, 'Come.' Let anyone who hears this say, 'Come.' Let anyone who is thirsty come. Let anyone who desires drink freely from the water of life" (Revelation 22:17). Money cannot buy salvation, and it cannot buy rescue from judgment. "Riches won't help on the day of judgment, but right living can save you from death" (Proverbs 11:4).

(7) Materialism spawns independence and self-sufficiency

Why trust God when you have all your bases covered? Why pray when you have everything under control? Why ask God for your daily bread when you own the bakery? We pride ourselves on our "financial independence," but where would we be without God, who gives every breath as a gift? Wealth insulates us from discerning the true depth of our need.

God warned his people, before they even set foot in the Promised Land, that the prosperity he intended to give them would actually turn them away from him. "I will bring them into the land I swore to give their ancestors—a land flowing with milk and honey. There they will become prosperous, eat all the food they want, and become fat. But they will begin to worship other gods; they will despise me and break my covenant" (Deuteronomy 31:20).

Hosea, watching both the northern and southern kingdoms explode in prosperity and yet implode spiritually, warned, "Israel has forgotten its Maker and built great palaces, and Judah has fortified its cities. Therefore, I will send down fire on their cities and will burn up their fortresses. . . . I have been the LORD your God ever since I brought you out of Egypt. You must acknowledge no God but me, for there is no other savior. I took care of you in the wilderness, in that dry and thirsty land. But when you had eaten and were satisfied, you became proud and forgot me" (Hosea 8:14; 13:4-6).

(8) Materialism leads to pride and elitism

The Bible is full of references proving that our tendency in prosperity is to believe we deserve credit for what we have and to grow proud and thankless. "Look what happens to mighty warriors who do not trust in God. They trust their wealth instead and grow more and more bold in their wickedness" (Psalm 52:7).

On the contrary, God is the one who has given us our intellect (Daniel 2:21), our abilities (Romans

12:6), and our capacity to earn money (Deuteronomy 8:18, NIV).

Jesus came to die for people of every social and economic level. Elitism boosts our egos by making us think we are somehow more worthy than others. Few things are more repugnant to the Lord than the rich despising the poor (Job 12:5; James 2:1-9). Yet our clubs and social circles, sometimes even our churches, can foster this very attitude.

(9) Materialism promotes injustice and exploitation

The Old Testament prophets spoke out often against the oppression of the poor by the rich. "You trample the poor, stealing their grain through taxes and unfair rent" (Amos 5:11). Micah warned, "The rich among you have become wealthy through extortion and violence. Your citizens are so used to lying that their tongues can no longer tell the truth" (Micah 6:12).

Rich people will usually be materialistic. So will poor people, but because they have less, usually what they have will exert less power over them. Materialistic people will be unjust. The wealthier the man, the greater his opportunity for injustice. Of course, the wealthy man is no more inherently sinful than the poor—he simply has more means and opportunity to fuel and impose sin upon others.

We shouldn't forget that historically, not long ago, slavery was a standard practice in America, and people in both the North and the South profited from it. But we need not go back 160 years to find notorious examples of exploitation. Consider today's profit-based abortion business, which is lucrative for the abortionist and financially advantageous to those parents who don't want to spend their time and money to care for a child or who fear they may jeopardize their careers or their house or car payments.

Consider also how promoters of alcohol, tobacco, drugs, pornography, prostitution, sensationalist tabloid journalism, and—in some cases—television and motion pictures exploit human beings for financial gain.

(10) Materialism fosters immorality and the deterioration of the family

Materialism underlies the vast majority of illegal activities. We shouldn't be surprised by the frequency of immorality among Christians—including Christian leaders—who live in great wealth. *After all, those who indulge their material appetites are not likely to curb their sexual appetites.*

King David, spoiled by getting everything he wanted, did not deny himself one more possession—another man's wife (2 Samuel 11:2-4). The biggest temptation for leaders, whether business, political, or spiritual, is to think they're an exception to the rule, that they're entitled to certain privileges "other people" are not.

But most forms of materialism are perfectly legal, and many enjoy the highest status, evoking admiration and envy. Don't misunderstand. A Christian can make millions of dollars a year, give generously, live modestly, and avoid much of the temptation to act immorally faced by most wealthy people. It's not how much money we make that grabs hold of our hearts. It's how much we keep.

CHAPTER 7

Battling Materialism in Christian Families

SCRIPTURE STATES THAT it is the responsibility of parents to provide for their children. For Christians to choose not to provide for their children or truly needy relatives is to deny the faith and become worse than an unbeliever (1 Timothy 5:8, 16). Likewise, it's the responsibility of grown children, not the state or an insurance company, to take care of their parents and other relatives in their old age or illness.

Jesus rejects any "spiritual" attempts to excuse a failure to provide materially for one's family (Mark 7:9-13). Christ, even when on the cross dying for the sins of the world, took the time to entrust his mother's welfare to one of his own apostles—who from that point forward made sure her needs were cared for (John 19:26-27).

What is "affluenza"?

It's one thing to provide for our children. It's another thing to smother them with possessions until they turn into self-centered materialists. An alarming number of children from Christian homes grow up grasping for every item they can lay their hands on. Children raised in such an atmosphere—which includes most children in America—are afflicted with a killer disease called "affluenza."

Children raised in wealth show many symptoms of those raised in abject poverty, including depression and anxiety. They experience despair, sometimes attempting suicide. They turn to alcohol, drugs, and shoplifting. Their parents are often so busy making money and spending it that they have little meaningful time with their children. They give them everything that money can buy, but money can't buy what's truly precious (Hebrews 13:5).

Consider the typical American Christmas. When the annual obstacle course through crowded malls culminates on the Big Day, what's the fruit? We find a trail of shredded wrapping paper and a pile of broken, abandoned, and unappreciated toys. Far from being filled with a spirit of thankfulness for all that Christmas means, children are often grabby, crabby, picky, sullen, and ungrateful—precisely because they've been given so much.

Things we would have deeply appreciated in small or moderate amounts become unappealing in excess. As a man who has gorged himself at a banquet finds the thought of food repulsive, one glutted with material things loses his regard and respect for them. The prevalent disrespect of children for their possessions and those of others is a direct result of overindulgence.

Children who grow up getting most of what they want have a predictable future. Unless they learn to overcome their upbringing, they'll misuse credit, default on their debts, and be poor employees. They'll function as irresponsible members of their family, church, and society. They'll be quick to blame others, pout about misfortunes, and believe that their family, church, country, and employer—if they have one—owe them.

Parents and grandparents who spoil children out of "love" should realize that by overindulging them, they are performing acts of child abuse. Although there are no laws against such abuse—no man-made laws, anyway—this spiritual mistreatment may result in as much long-term personal and social damage as the worst physical abuse.

Is there any substitute for a parent?

Every good financial perspective or habit encouraged in this book is developed best by the example of parents. Children learn most effectively not only from what we say but from what we do. Sometimes our actions speak so loudly that our children can't hear a word we're saying.

Training our children about money and possessions begins at birth (Proverbs 22:6). For better or worse, we are their tutors, every hour of every day. Albert Schweitzer put it this way: "There are only three ways to teach a child. The first is by example; the second is by example; the third is by example."

Giving gifts to children is often a substitute for giving them personal attention. Many children receive a playhouse, then a train set, then skis, then a motorcycle, then a car, all to compensate for the fact that their parents—often their father in particular—are not available to spend time with them. Anything we give our children is a poor substitute for ourselves.

I spoke with a Christian man who loves his wife and five children and wants the best for them. He works hard so they can have a beautiful house, lots of things, and enough money for the children to go to college. In fact, he works so hard that the last three years he hasn't had time to go on vacation with his family! This man's children are growing up with plenty of material things. Tragically, they're also growing up without a father.

Our children will not remember what we did *for* them nearly as much as they'll remember what we did *with* them.

No man on his deathbed will look back and wish he had spent less time with his children.

What about our children's other teachers?

Society is much more aggressive in teaching our children about money than we are. For an educational experience, spend a Saturday morning watching cartoons and children's programs. Take special note of the commercials. Advertising goes straight to the kids, inundating them with a materialistic perspective and subtly encouraging them to manipulate their parents into buying trendy products.

Although some parents and grandparents, including me, are rightly concerned about the sexual values taught by television, equally dangerous are the material values. We can develop our children's discernment and decision-making skills by asking them on the spot what an advertisement is saying and what its purpose really is. Ask them, "How important do you think these things are to God?" and "How would they improve your character or spiritual life if you owned them?" Don't dismiss these ads as silly—discuss them with your children. Only with dialogue and training can they learn to discern the faulty underpinnings of society's insistent materialism.

Surrounded by so much unbiblical instruction about money, we parents need strong allies. There's much that our churches can do to teach basic biblical principles of stewardship to children, youth, and adults. Sermons, classes, special seminars, small-group discussions, parent support groups, family-oriented radio programs, books, CDs, and DVDs—all these are potential tools to challenge and equip parents.

How about a field trip to a dump?

How can we teach our children the emptiness of materialism in a direct and memorable way? Try taking them to visit a junkyard or a dump. (The lines are shorter than at amusement parks, admission is free, and little boys love it.) Show them all the piles of "treasures" that were formerly Christmas and birthday presents. Point out things that cost hundreds of dollars, children quarreled about, friendships were lost over, honesty was sacrificed for, and marriages broken up over. Show them the miscellaneous remnants of battered dolls, rusted robots, and electronic gadgets that now lie useless after their brief life span. Point out to them that most of what your family owns will one day end up in a junkyard like this. Read 2 Peter 3:10-14, which tells us that everything in this world will be consumed by fire. Then ask them this question: When all that we owned lies abandoned, broken, and useless, what will we have done with our lives that will last for eternity?

CHAPTER 8

Rethinking Prosperity Theology (Hint: God Is Not Our Genie)

THIS IS THE final chapter on those deeply entrenched worldviews that poison our thinking and impede faithful financial stewardship. And for some Christians, this one is the most dangerous of all—"prosperity theology," also known as the "health and wealth gospel."

This philosophy teaches that the more money you give away, the wealthier you will become. Following God through giving and other forms of obedience becomes a formula for abundant provision and the celebration of prosperous living. This is, in essence, a Christianized materialism.

What distinguishes prosperity theology from secular materialism is that it professes to be built on God's Word. That is precisely what makes it most dangerous. Heresies are hazardous because of the bits of truth they contain. Prosperity theology is like chocolate-covered rat poison. Without its truth-coating, many believers wouldn't swallow its lies.

Doesn't God promise to make us prosperous if we obey him?

The portion of truth that makes prosperity theology credible is that some Old Testament passages do indeed link material prosperity with God's blessing. For instance, God gave material wealth to Abraham (Genesis 13:1-6), Isaac (26:12-14), Jacob (30:43), Joseph (41:41-43), Solomon (1 Kings 3:13), and Job (Job 42:10-17) because he approved of them. He promised the Israelites that he would reward them materially for faithful financial giving (Deuteronomy 15:10; Proverbs 3:9-10; 11:25; Malachi 3:8-12).

But this is by no means the whole picture. God warns against the dangers of wealth—especially that in prosperity people often forget the Lord (Deuteronomy 8:7-18). But even when people love God with all their hearts, they suffer. In fact, they're promised suffering (Acts 14:22; 2 Timothy 3:12).

Job laments, "Why do the wicked prosper, growing old and powerful? They live to see their children grow up and settle down, and they enjoy their grandchildren. Their homes are safe from every fear, and God does not punish them. . . . They spend their days in prosperity" (Job 21:7-9, 13).

The psalmist asks, "LORD, how long will the wicked, how long will the wicked triumph?" (Psalm 94:3, NKJV).

Jeremiah, a righteous man who lived in constant adversity, framed the question this way: "LORD, you always give me justice when I bring a case before you. So let me bring you this complaint: Why are the wicked so prosperous? Why are evil people so happy?" (Jeremiah 12:1).

If, as prosperity theology maintains, material wealth is a reliable indicator of God's reward and approval, then crime bosses, embezzlers, and drug lords are the apple of his eye. History is full of successful madmen and prosperous despots. If, on the other hand, lack of wealth always shows his disapproval, then Jesus and Paul were on God's blacklist.

Jesus reminds us that his common grace is available to all, for our Father "gives his sunlight to both the evil and the good, and he sends rain on the just and the unjust alike" (Matthew 5:45). Similarly, he sends both prosperity and hardship on those who obey him and those who disobey.

What about Job and Lazarus and godly people who suffer?

Many in Old and New Testament times believed in a direct cause-and-effect relationship between righteousness and prosperity on the one hand, and sin and adversity on the other. Job's "comforters" thought there must be hidden sin in his life to account for his loss of prosperity, but they were wrong. God approved of Job (Job 1:8; 42:7), yet he permitted Satan to destroy everything of earthly value that Job possessed and allowed his children to die.

The well-to-do Pharisees lived and breathed prosperity theology, labeling everyone beneath their social caste as "sinners" (Luke 15:1-2; John 9:34). Christ's disciples betrayed their assumptions when they asked, "Rabbi, who sinned, this man or his parents, that he was born blind?" (John 9:2, NIV). Jesus responded by saying their presupposition was faulty: "'Neither this man nor his parents sinned,' said Jesus, 'but this happened so that the works of God might be displayed in him'" (verse 3, NIV). In other words, God had a higher purpose for this man's adversity that didn't fit into the neat little boxes of "Do good and you'll prosper" and "Do bad and you'll suffer."

What we call prosperity is often incidental. As Christ's account of the rich man and Lazarus demonstrates, an evil person may live long, suffer little, and prosper much, while the righteous person may suffer much, live with disease, and die in poverty (Luke 16:19-25). Jesus says things will be turned around in eternity, but often not until then. In the present life, the righteous can suffer and the wicked can prosper.

> God blesses you who are poor, for the
> Kingdom of God is yours. God blesses you
> who are hungry now, for you will be satisfied.
> God blesses you who weep now, for in due
> time you will laugh. What blessings await you
> when people hate you and exclude you and
> mock you and curse you as evil because you
> follow the Son of Man. When that happens,

be happy! Yes, leap for joy! For a great reward awaits you in heaven. And remember, their ancestors treated the ancient prophets that same way. What sorrow awaits you who are rich, for you have your only happiness now. What sorrow awaits you who are fat and prosperous now, for a time of awful hunger awaits you. What sorrow awaits you who laugh now, for your laughing will turn to mourning and sorrow. What sorrow awaits you who are praised by the crowds, for their ancestors also praised false prophets. (Luke 6:20-26)

Prosperity or persecution?

Not only may the righteous suffer despite their righteousness, but often they will suffer *because* of their righteousness. The early Christians continually suffered for their faith. A materialistic world system, with its emphasis on personal peace and prosperity, does not look with favor upon a true disciple of Christ. The following examples from Scripture should disturb any of us whose goal is to be hailed a success by the standards of this world:

- "Everyone who wants to live a godly life in Christ Jesus will suffer persecution. But evil people and impostors will flourish. They will deceive others and will themselves be deceived" (2 Timothy 3:12-13).

- "For you have been given not only the privilege
  of trusting in Christ but also the privilege of
  suffering for him" (Philippians 1:29).
- "If the world hates you, remember that it hated
  me first. The world would love you as one of its
  own if you belonged to it, but you are no longer
  part of the world. I chose you to come out of
  the world, so it hates you. Do you remember
  what I told you? 'A slave is not greater than the
  master.' Since they persecuted me, naturally
  they will persecute you. And if they had
  listened to me, they would listen to you" (John
  15:18-20).

If we fit in so well with the world, is it because we're
living by the world's standards, instead of Christ's?

There's great irony in a popular "health and wealth"
saying: "Live like a King's kid." Well, the foremost
"King's kid" was Jesus, who lived a life exactly oppo-
site of what is meant by the phrase today. How did
the King send his "kid" into this world? Born in lowly
Bethlehem, raised in despised Nazareth, part of a pious
but poor family that offered two doves because they
couldn't afford a lamb to sacrifice (Leviticus 12:6-8;
Luke 2:22-24). Christ wandered the countryside
dependent on others to open their homes because he
didn't have one of his own. "Live like a King's kid"?
Whatever "king's kid" the prosperity proponents are
speaking of, it obviously isn't Jesus!

Prosperity theology sees as our model the ascended

heavenly Lord rather than the descended earthly servant. Jesus warned his disciples not to follow a lordship model but his own servant model (Mark 10:42-45). In this life, we are to share his cross—in the next life we will share his crown (2 Timothy 2:12).

What can we learn about prosperity theology from the apostle Paul?

Raised a Pharisee and therefore a believer in prosperity theology, Paul was one of those who couldn't believe that Jesus was Messiah. Surely God's disapproval of the man Jesus was self-evident in his questionable parentage, his disreputable hometown of Nazareth, his lack of formal education, his poverty, and above all, his shameful death. But when Paul bowed his knee to the Carpenter from Galilee, he forever turned his back on prosperity theology. As his Lord said, "I will show him how much he must suffer for my name's sake" (Acts 9:16).

In Philippians 3:7-8, Paul discusses his credentials of success, his diplomas and awards: "I once thought these things were valuable, but now I consider them worthless because of what Christ has done. Yes, everything else is worthless when compared with the infinite value of knowing Christ Jesus my Lord. For his sake I have discarded everything else, counting it all as garbage, so that I could gain Christ."

Paul called his credentials of success and his possessions garbage, or more literally, excrement. As a result of following Christ, Paul lost everything. He faced off with prosperity preachers, pointing out that by living as kings now, rather than as servants, they were attempting to rush their reign with Christ. His point was clear: Wait for God to hand out the crowns based on his appraisal of our faithfulness as we humbly serve.

Our attitude should be as Paul described in his letter to the church in Corinth: "We serve God whether people honor us or despise us, whether they slander us or praise us. We are honest, but they call us impostors. We are ignored, even though we are well known. We live close to death, but we are still alive. We have been beaten, but we have not been killed. Our hearts ache, but we always have joy. We are poor, but we give spiritual riches to others. We own nothing, and yet we have everything" (2 Corinthians 6:8-10).

The distorted worldview Paul confronted in the first century is still with us today, and it's called the "*health* and wealth gospel" for a reason—it integrates both together.

Paul wrote what no health and wealth gospel preacher would: "To keep me from becoming proud, I was given a thorn in my flesh, a messenger from Satan to torment me and keep me from becoming proud. Three different times I begged the Lord to take it away. Each time he said, 'My grace is all you need. My power works best in weakness.' So now I am glad to boast about my weaknesses, so that the power of Christ can work through me. That's why I take pleasure in my weaknesses, and in the insults, hardships, persecutions, and troubles that I suffer for Christ. For when I am weak, then I am strong" (2 Corinthians 12:7-10).

Whatever Paul's affliction, it was "given" to him by God, who had a specific purpose for not removing it—to teach Paul that he wasn't to trust in his own strength but in God's.

We need to recognize that God may accomplish higher purposes through our sickness than our health. Certainly we should follow Paul's example and pray for healing, but notice that he prayed only three times. When God chose not to heal him, Paul didn't "name it and claim it" and demand healing. Instead, he acknowledged God's spiritual purpose in his adversity.

If you've prayed for healing and have not received it, take heart—you're in good company! Not only was Paul himself not healed, but he also had to leave his friend Trophimus in Miletus because of sickness (2 Timothy 4:20). His son in the faith, Timothy, had frequent stomach disorders. Paul didn't tell him to "claim healing" but to drink a little wine for medicinal purposes (1 Timothy 5:23). Those who declare "anyone with enough faith can be healed" must think they have greater faith than Paul and his missionary associates.

Like many of God's servants in the early church, Paul was neither healthy nor wealthy. Of course Paul *now* enjoys perfect health and wealth. God does promise unending health and wealth to all his people. But that promise will be fulfilled in the Resurrection and on the New Earth (Revelation 21:4).

So why *does* God prosper us sometimes?

I have no argument with anyone who says that God often prospers his people materially. By no means always, yet often he does. But the great question is this: What does he expect us to do with that abundance? Health and wealth preachers suggest that we may do whatever we please with God's provision. We may buy beautiful homes and cars, take dream vacations, and live in wealth and prosperity—as long as we give God the credit. Some prosperity preachers declare that God expects us—even *commands* us—to live in luxury so that we are not "bad witnesses" by appearing to be poor! By this standard, Jesus and Paul were terrible witnesses.

God entrusts riches to us, not so we can keep them, but so we can *give* them: "God will generously provide all you need. Then you will always have everything you need and plenty left over to share with others. . . . Yes, you will be enriched in every way so that you can always be generous" (2 Corinthians 9:8, 11).

Beyond what we need, which God generously provides, Paul says we will have "plenty left over to share with others." That seems to be a clear statement about why God gives us plenty—not to find a new way to spend it but to find the right place to give it. Augustine put it this way: "Find out how much God has given you and from it take what you need; the remainder is needed by others."

Giving away money puts us in a position of financial weakness. We don't like that—we prefer helping the sick and poor from a position of health and wealth. But giving away our excess does something for us that keeping or spending it doesn't. It makes us dependent on God and keeps us open to the possibility that at some point we may need to depend on others, just as they are currently depending on us. "Right now you have plenty and can help those who are in need. Later, they will have plenty and can share with you when you need it. In this way, things will be equal" (2 Corinthians 8:14).

Christ said, "Do to others whatever you would like them to do to you" (Matthew 7:12). If you and your children were hungry, what would you want prosperous Christians to do for you? If your answer is "share their abundance with our family," then just say no to prosperity theology, obey Christ, and share generously with those in need.

Our Stewardship in Eternity's Light

CHAPTER 9

Two Treasuries, Two Perspectives, Two Masters: Choosing between Two Kingdoms

HAVING DEALT WITH the barriers to thinking correctly about money and possessions, we now turn our attention to seeing our work as God's money managers through the lens of eternity. The three chapters in this section are of great importance. Why? Because only when we look at our lives with an eternal perspective will we be able to make eternally wise, countercultural choices that may not be easy today but will pay off in the long tomorrow.

How do we keep money and possessions in perspective?

Jesus told us where we should place our treasures and our hearts.

> Do not store up for yourselves treasures on earth, where moth and rust destroy, and where thieves break in and steal. But store up for

yourselves treasures in heaven, where moth
and rust do not destroy, and where thieves
do not break in and steal. For where your
treasure is, there your heart will be also. The
eye is the lamp of the body. If your eyes are
good, your whole body will be full of light.
But if your eyes are bad, your whole body will
be full of darkness. If then the light within
you is darkness, how great is that darkness!
No one can serve two masters. Either he will
hate the one and love the other, or he will be
devoted to the one and despise the other. You
cannot serve both God and money. (Matthew
6:19-24, NIV)

Jesus presents three groups of two. *Two treasures*:
the present Earth and the future Heaven. *Two perspectives*: the good eye and the bad eye. *Two masters*: God
and money.

Money is only of temporary value—unless, that is,
it's used and spent and shared and given with a view
toward heavenly treasure. Moths destroy fabric, rust
corrodes "precious" metals, and thieves can steal almost
anything. Jesus could have gone on—fires consume,
floods inundate, governments seize, enemies attack,
investments tank. *No earthly treasure is safe.*

Material things just won't stand the test of time.
Even if they escape moths and rust and thieves,
they cannot escape the coming fire of God that will
consume the material world (2 Peter 3:7). Christ's

primary argument against amassing material wealth isn't that it's morally wrong but simply that it's a poor investment.

Financial planners try to convince people to look ahead instead of focusing on today or this month. "Think thirty years from now," they'll say. Then they'll share ways to do that by planning, budgeting, saving, contributing to an IRA, investing in this mutual fund or that real estate partnership.

But the truth is, thinking thirty years ahead is only slightly less shortsighted than thinking thirty days ahead. Christ, the ultimate investment counselor, says, "Don't ask how your investment will be paying off in just thirty years. Ask how it will be paying off in thirty *million* years." Wise people, according to Jesus, think ahead not just to their retirement years but to *eternity*. Treasures on Earth last a short time; treasures in Heaven last forever.

When Jesus speaks of the eyes, he refers to perspective. What he calls the "bad eye" was in Jewish culture the "evil eye" that envies others, covets what's theirs, and wishes harm to them. The Christian's perspective on wealth, seen through the "good eye," looks at wealth with eternal perspective. It sees temporary earthly treasures not only as God's provision for us but as a means to serve God and help others, and in the process store up eternal treasures in Heaven. We gratefully use money to care for ourselves and sometimes to save and invest and build a business. But even as we do this, we see it for what it is—something useful but temporary, which if overvalued and overaccumulated, will take control of our lives.

Having spoken of two treasuries and two perspectives, Jesus speaks finally of two masters. He says that although we might *have* both God and money, we cannot *serve* both God and money. There's a throne in each life big enough for only one. Christ may be on that throne. Money may be on that throne. But both cannot occupy it.

Jesus is telling us that we should spend our lives investing in the right treasury, adopting the right perspective, and serving the right master.

What does it mean to store up treasures in Heaven?

We store up treasures on Earth by accumulating and gripping them tightly. We store up treasures in Heaven by holding loosely, sharing freely, and giving away earthly treasures for God's Kingdom purposes.

What reason does Christ give for storing up treasures in Heaven rather than on Earth? Jesus doesn't say to do it because it's right but because it's *smart*. Because such treasures will *last*, Jesus argues from the bottom line. It's not an emotional appeal; it's a logical one: *Invest in what has lasting value.*

You'll never see a hearse pulling a U-Haul. Why? *Because you can't take it with you.*

God tells us, "Don't be dismayed when the wicked grow rich and their homes become ever more splendid.

For when they die, they take nothing with them. Their wealth will not follow them into the grave" (Psalm 49:16-17).

Again, *you can't take it with you.*

John D. Rockefeller was one of the wealthiest men who ever lived. After he died, someone asked his accountant, "How much money did John D. leave?" His reply was classic: "He left . . . *all* of it."

Once more: *You can't take it with you.*

If that point is clear in your mind, you're ready to see the paradigm-shifting significance of what Jesus is saying in Matthew 6. He takes that profound truth "You can't take it with you" and adds a stunning qualification. By telling us to store up treasures for ourselves in Heaven, Jesus is saying, "You can't take it with you— but you can send it on ahead."

In my book by the same name, I call this "the treasure principle." And if it doesn't take your breath away, you've missed the point! Anything we try to hang on to here is temporary treasure that will be lost. But anytime we put earthly treasures into God's hands, we store up eternal treasures for ourselves in Heaven.

If we give instead of keep, we invest in the eternal instead of in the temporal, we store up treasures in Heaven that will never stop paying dividends. Whatever treasures we store up on Earth will be left behind when we die. Whatever treasures we store up in Heaven will be waiting for us when we arrive.

Of course, there are many good things God wants us to do with money that don't involve giving it away.

It's essential, for instance, that we provide for our family's basic material needs (1 Timothy 5:8). But these good things are only a beginning. The money God entrusts to us here on Earth is eternal investment capital. Every day is an opportunity to buy up more shares in his Kingdom.

Ponder it: *You can't take it with you, but you can send it on ahead.*

It's a revolutionary concept. If you embrace it, I guarantee it will change your life.

Notice that Jesus *wants* us to store up our treasures. He's just telling us to stop storing them in the wrong place—on Earth where they won't last—and start storing them in the right place—in Heaven, where they'll last forever!

And isn't it remarkable that Jesus said, "Store up *for yourselves* treasures in heaven"? Does it seem strange that Jesus commands us to do what's in our own best interest? Wouldn't that be selfish? No. God expects and commands us to act out of enlightened self-interest. He wants us to live for his glory, but what is for his glory is always for our good. As John Piper puts it, "God is most glorified in us when we are most satisfied in him."

Selfishness is when we pursue gain at the expense of others. But God doesn't have a limited number of treasures to distribute. When you store up treasures for yourself in Heaven, it does not reduce the treasures available to others. In fact, it is by serving God and others that we store up heavenly treasures. So everyone gains, and no one loses.

Is storing up treasures in Heaven really about giving?

Some have told me they don't believe that Jesus is speaking about giving when he commands us to store up treasures in Heaven rather than on Earth. But both the immediate context and the parallel passages make it clear that giving is primarily what he's talking about.

In Matthew 6:1-4 (NIV), before speaking about treasures on Earth and in Heaven, Jesus tells his disciples not to seek reward from men for their giving, for then "you will have no reward from your Father in heaven." He adds that if they do their giving (and fasting and praying) for God and not men, "your Father, who sees what is done in secret, will reward you." Jesus establishes a clear theme: God rewards his children for practicing the spiritual disciplines, the first being giving.

When we surrender our earthly treasures to care for the needy, love our neighbor, and further the purposes of God, he rewards us. How? The passage goes on to tell us—by turning those earthly treasures into heavenly ones.

Jesus not only *precedes* his words about storing treasures in Heaven by referring specifically to giving away money, he *follows* them by calling money a false god, another master (Matthew 6:24). We serve money as master when we hold on to it as our treasure. We topple the money idol by giving away money and material things, storing up treasures in Heaven.

But even if someone concludes the immediate context of the command to store up treasures in Heaven isn't sufficient to prove it refers to giving, its parallel passages leave no doubt. Consider this: "Sell your possessions, and give to the needy. Provide yourselves with moneybags that do not grow old, with a treasure in the heavens that does not fail, where no thief approaches and no moth destroys. For where your treasure is, there will your heart be also" (Luke 12:33-34, ESV).

Christ explicitly says that selling our possessions and giving the money to the needy produces "treasure in the heavens that does not fail." There is no ambiguity here: *Financial giving stores up eternal treasures in Heaven.*

And if the parallel passage in Luke isn't enough, Mark quotes Jesus as saying, "Go, sell everything you have and give to the poor, and you will have treasure in heaven" (Mark 10:21, NIV). There it is: Giving away money and possessions to the poor results directly in treasures in Heaven. How could it possibly be clearer?

Not only do Mark and Luke establish a definitive connection between giving and storing up treasures in Heaven, so does the apostle Paul. He alludes directly to Christ's words in the Gospels when he writes to Timothy about the rich: "Tell them to use their money to do good. They should be rich in good works and *generous to those in need*, always being *ready to share with others*. By doing this they will be *storing up their treasure as a good foundation for the future* so that they may experience true life" (1 Timothy 6:18-19).

Paul knew what Jesus was talking about when he commanded us to store up treasures in Heaven, which is why he used his exact terminology. We do it by giving generously to the needy.

Despite this overwhelming interpretive evidence, some commentaries on Matthew 6:19-24 speak in remarkably vague terms about Christ wanting us to be Kingdom-minded and say nothing about giving away money and possessions as a means by which we are to store up treasures in Heaven. Certainly the passage would be less countercultural and far easier to fulfill if it merely required good thoughts on our part, not radical acts of generosity. But culture and convenience shouldn't dictate interpretation.

Of course, Christ's words about storing up treasures in Heaven can be broadly applied to how we spend our time and use our abilities. But the central emphasis of the text, which the apostles understood, is about giving money and possessions. As Craig Blomberg states in the *New American Commentary on Matthew*, "In this context, however, storing up treasures focuses particularly on the compassionate use of material resources to meet others' physical and spiritual needs, in keeping with the priorities of God's kingdom."

What is an eternal investment?

Christ's position on wealth is not that it should be rejected but that it should be pursued. *True wealth is worth seeking.*

So what constitutes true wealth? By putting our money and possessions in Christ's treasury while we're still on Earth, we assure ourselves of eternal rewards beyond comprehension: "The Kingdom of Heaven is like a treasure that a man discovered hidden in a field. In his excitement, he hid it again and sold everything he owned to get enough money to buy the field. Again, the Kingdom of Heaven is like a merchant on the lookout for choice pearls. When he discovered a pearl of great value, he sold everything he owned and bought it!" (Matthew 13:44-46).

Consider the implications of this offer. We can trade temporal possessions we can't keep to gain eternal possessions we can't lose. This is like a child trading a broken whistle for a new bicycle or a man accepting majority stock in Coca-Cola in exchange for a sack of bottle caps. Only a fool would pass up the opportunity.

I use this analogy in my book *The Treasure Principle: Discovering the Secret of Joyful Giving*:

Imagine you're alive at the end of the Civil War. You're living in the South, but you're a Northerner. You plan to move home as soon as the war's over. While in the South you've accumulated lots of Confederate currency. Now, suppose you know for a fact the North's going to win the war, and the end is imminent. What will you do with your Confederate money?

If you're smart, there's only one answer. You should immediately cash in your Confederate currency for U.S. currency—the only money that will have value once the war's over. Keep only enough Confederate currency to meet your short-term needs.

Kingdom currency is the only medium of exchange recognized by the Son of God, whose government will last forever. That currency is our present faithful service and sacrificial use of our resources for him.

When the Lord returns, what will happen to all the money sitting in bank accounts, retirement programs, estates, and foundations? It will burn like wood, hay, and straw, when it could have been used to feed the hungry and fulfill the great commission.

Suppose with $20,000 I could buy a new car. With the same money, I could help translate the Scriptures for an unreached people group, support church planting, feed the hungry in the name of Christ, facilitate gospel literature distribution in Southeast Asia, or support full-time multiple missionary families in parts of the world for a year. If I have an investment mentality, I ask myself, *What's the better investment for eternity?*

True, a car used for God's purposes can also be an investment in the Kingdom. But I must be careful not to rationalize. A used car or no car at all may serve his Kingdom purposes equally well or far better—and allow me to make an investment in Heaven that will never get scratched, dented, stolen, or totaled. And if I invest the money in his Kingdom and ask him to provide a car at little or no expense, might he choose to do that? Shouldn't I give him the opportunity?

People are always looking for safe places to put their money. Jesus says there's ultimately only one place where it will never go up in smoke: the Kingdom of God. Once given away to the Christ-centered cause, once removed from our hands and placed fully in God's hands, it remains forever safe.

As he considers his approaching death, Paul describes this eternal investment to Timothy: "As for me, my life has already been poured out as an offering to God. The time of my death is near. I have fought the good fight, I have finished the race, and I have remained faithful. And now the prize awaits me—the crown of righteousness, which the Lord, the righteous Judge, will give me on the day of his return. And the prize is not just for me but for all who eagerly look forward to his appearing" (2 Timothy 4:6-8).

Where do we find the motivation to invest eternally?

Peter encouraged Christians to find joy by focusing not on the trial that will go on only "a little while" but on their heavenly inheritance that will never perish. As missionary martyr Jim Elliot put it, "He is no fool who gives what he cannot keep to gain what he cannot lose." Why work for what has no lasting value? Why rejoice over what in the end will not matter?

God tells us, "We have a priceless inheritance—an inheritance that is kept in heaven for you, pure and undefiled, beyond the reach of change and decay" (1 Peter 1:4).

In times of suffering, we must remember what is awaiting us in eternity with Christ. Romans 8:18 says, "What we suffer now is nothing compared to the glory he will reveal to us later." Second Corinthians 4:17 promises, "Our present troubles are small and won't last very long. Yet they produce for us a glory that vastly outweighs them and will last forever!"

Though the glory of Christ is precious above all, Christ also promises a derivative glory for his people that we will experience in Heaven. Some say Christ should be our *only* treasure. The Bible says Christ should be our *primary* treasure. When God commands us to store up treasures for ourselves, that doesn't mean we are to store up *christs* for ourselves (which it would have to mean if he were our only treasure). Christ is not our only treasure, but also the Treasure above and behind all treasures.

Note also that Jesus does not say, "Store up for God treasures in heaven"; he said, "Store up *for yourselves* treasures in heaven" (Matthew 6:20, NIV). This may sound selfish, but it is Christ's command to us, so we should eagerly obey it. Christ's promise of eternal rewards for our present stewardship choices gives the believer an incentive to do what the Philippian Christians did in giving to Paul's missionary work— withdrawing funds from their earthly accounts to deposit them into ventures with eternal value. "Not that I am looking for a gift, but I am looking for what may be credited to your account" (Philippians 4:17, NIV). Once again, Paul is speaking about depositing treasures in Heaven by generous Kingdom giving.

Suppose I offer you $1,000 to spend today however you want. Not a bad deal. But suppose I give you a choice—you can either have that $1,000 today, or you can have $10 million if you'll wait one year—then $10 million more every year thereafter. What will you choose? Only a fool would take the $1,000 today.

A year might seem a long time to wait for the payoff. But after it passes, wouldn't you be grateful you waited? Likewise, won't we be far more grateful in Heaven that we chose to forego earthly treasures in order to enjoy forever the treasures we sent ahead?

This is delayed gratification. Soldiers, athletes, and farmers all know that long-term benefits justify short-term sacrifices (2 Timothy 2:3-6). The same principle applies to those who live in light of eternity. Only when we adopt an eternal perspective will we eagerly follow our Lord's command to devote our brief lives on Earth to the pursuit of eternal treasure.

CHAPTER 10

God's Steward's Eternal Destiny: Heaven

A STARTLING THING has happened among Western Christians. Many of us habitually think and act as if no eternity awaits us. How many sermons about Heaven or Hell have most of us heard lately? How many modern gospel booklets even mention the words *Heaven* or *Hell*? How many Christian books talk about everything else but Heaven and Hell?

The trend is to focus on our present circumstances instead of our eternal future. Yet Peter explains that eternal realities should influence the character of our present life, right down to every word we speak and every action we take. "Since everything around us is going to be destroyed like this, what holy and godly lives you should live" (2 Peter 3:11).

Those who don't have a biblical understanding of the wonders in store for us in God's resurrected universe often think of it as dreamlike, so otherworldly as to be unreal. So they come back to "reality"—their present lives and possessions that they can see, hear, touch, feel, and taste.

Being oblivious to eternity leaves us experts in the trivial and novices in the significant. We can name that tune, name that starting lineup, name that actor's movie debut, and debate the differences between Windows and Mac platforms. None of this is wrong, of course, but it's revealing when we consider that most Christians, let alone the general public, do not have an accurate picture of what the Bible says will happen to us after we die.

Why is it important to view our present lives through the lens of eternity?

The Bible is clear: Life is short. James reminds his readers, "How do you know what your life will be like tomorrow? Your life is like the morning fog—it's here a little while, then it's gone" (James 4:14).

A cynical saying exposes the futility of heaping up wealth: "He who dies with the most toys wins." But in fact, he still dies, and he wins nothing. Does anyone wish to be known as the richest person in the cemetery?

Eternity will hold for us what we have invested there during our life on Earth. According to Scripture, the central business of this life is preparing for the next! Remember: You can't take it with you, but you *can* send it on ahead.

Since you have been raised to new life with Christ, set your sights on the realities of heaven, where Christ sits in the place of honor at God's right hand. Think about the things of heaven, not the things of earth. For you died to this life, and your real life is hidden with Christ in God. And when Christ, who is your life, is revealed to the whole world, you will share in all his glory. (Colossians 3:1-4)

Is Heaven really a place we should look forward to?

Because I have written a number of books on the subject of Heaven and the New Earth, I have heard from thousands of Christians over the years. Many of them tell me that for most of their lives they have not thought of Heaven as a place to look forward to. They think of it as immaterial and ghostly and basically inhuman.

Every time Scripture speaks of Heaven, it portrays it as a real place inhabited by real people, not by ghosts or pale, neutered imps floating in the clouds. The Bible anticipates and focuses on the Resurrection, which is the antidote to all the vague, dull, and thoroughly unbiblical concepts about Heaven that cause us not to long for it, and even to dread it. We would do well to remind ourselves that "in your presence there is fullness of joy; at your right hand are pleasures forevermore" (Psalm 16:11, ESV).

Why talk about Heaven in a book on managing God's money? Because our misconceptions about Heaven, and our consequent lack of excitement about living there forever, feed into our shortsightedness and our habit of clinging to this fallen Earth as our home. Seeing Heaven as the Bible portrays it will help free us from materialism and encourage us to live in light of God's eternal Kingdom. We will bring an eternal perspective to our money management here and now only if we understand what awaits us in our eternal future.

For Christians, Heaven is our home. The capital of this heavenly country will be a "city with eternal foundations, a city designed and built by God" (Hebrews 11:10). This city will have all the freshness, vitality, and openness of the country with all the vibrancy, interdependence, and relationships of a city. A city without crime, litter, smog, sirens, seaminess, or slums. It will be "a country [we] can call [our] own" (verse 14), "a better place, a heavenly homeland" (verse 16).

Home is the place of acceptance, security, rest, refuge, deep personal relationships, and great memories.

Will we really eat and drink and spend time with friends?

When Christians die, our spirits go to the present Heaven. To be with Christ will make that place delightful beyond comprehension. Yet the Bible says that Christ will come down from Heaven to return to this world, bringing his people with him. We will experience resurrection, the joining of our spirits with new bodies. We will live as physical beings on a physical New Earth, in relationship with God and each other.

God will bring down a great city from Heaven and relocate his throne to the New Earth, where he will forever dwell with his people (Revelation 21:1-4; 22:3). In other words, God will bring Heaven to Earth.

Christ promises that after the Resurrection we will eat and drink with people from all over the planet: "I tell you this, that many Gentiles will come from all over the world—from east and west—and sit down with Abraham, Isaac, and Jacob at the feast in the Kingdom of Heaven" (Matthew 8:11).

We'll meet and converse with not only Abraham, Isaac, and Jacob, but Moses, David, Ruth, Esther, Mary, and Peter. Imagine conversations with C. S. Lewis, A. W. Tozer, Jonathan Edwards, and Amy Carmichael. I often think about this, and it always brings a smile to my face!

We'll also converse with angels. Because angels are ministering spirits who serve us (Hebrews 1:14), we'll presumably get to know those who protected us during our years on Earth. Perhaps we'll be invited into angels' quarters to visit with them in exchange for the hospitality we offered them in this life when we were unaware of their true identity (13:2).

Will we learn in Heaven? Definitely. Paul wrote that God "raised us up with him and seated us with him in the heavenly places in Christ Jesus, so that in the coming ages he might show the immeasurable riches of his grace in kindness toward us in Christ Jesus" (Ephesians 2:6-7, ESV).

When we die, we'll know a lot more than we do

now, but we'll keep learning about God and all he's done for us. I think we'll probably look back at our lives here in this fallen world and see God's kindness to us in events of our lives that may have seemed anything but kind. And if we'll learn more of God's gracious purposes in our lives, surely we'll discover more and more of his new creation and behold his glory more as a result, with breathtaking freshness and exhilaration.

God is *the* Creator, and he made his human image bearers to be creators. God gave Adam and Eve creativity in their unfallen state that remained, though twisted, when they fell. After the Resurrection, as we live with him on the New Earth (Revelation 21–22), surely God will not endow us with less creativity but *more*, a creativity unmarred by sin, unlimited by mortality. Surely, we should expect to design, build, compose, study, write, sculpt, plant, play, and explore.

Will we remember our lives and relationships on Earth? Of course. Remembrance is important to God, which is why the heavenly city has memorials of people and events on Earth—the apostles and tribes of Israel among them (Revelation 21:14).

It's also why God keeps in Heaven "a scroll of remembrance," written in his presence, "to record the names of those who feared him and always thought about the honor of his name" (Malachi 3:16). The pain of the past will be gone. But memories of being together in the trenches, walking with Christ, and experiencing intimate times with family and friends will remain.

The names written on the scrolls of Heaven will

remind us of the history of this world we live in. If God wanted us to forget this life, he surely wouldn't write down for prominent display the names of those who lived here and served him here.

Will we know our loved ones in Heaven? Certainly. We may immediately know even those we *didn't* know on Earth, just as Peter, James, and John recognized Moses and Elijah when they joined Jesus (Luke 9:28-33).

Certainly we'll get to know people, since we'll be smarter and healthier and enjoy relationships more than we do now. After entering Heaven, the martyrs look down on Earth and clearly remember their lives, fully aware of what's happening there.

When the Lamb broke the fifth seal, I saw under the altar the souls of all who had been martyred for the word of God and for being faithful in their testimony. They shouted to the Lord and said, "O Sovereign Lord, holy and true, how long before you judge the people who belong to this world and avenge our blood for what they have done to us?" Then a white robe was given to each of them. And they were told to rest a little longer until the full number of their brothers and sisters—their fellow servants of Jesus who were to be martyred—had joined them. (Revelation 6:9-11)

Heaven isn't a place of ignorance of events on Earth but of perspective concerning them.

Will we rest or work or both?

Heaven will offer much-needed rest to the weary. But rest renews us and revitalizes us to become active again. As there was work to do in Eden, before sin and the Curse on the ground, the New Earth will offer refreshing activity, productive and unthwarted.

Regarding rest, Scripture says, "I heard a voice from heaven saying, 'Write this down: Blessed are those who die in the Lord from now on. Yes, says the Spirit, they are blessed indeed, for they will rest from their hard work; for their good deeds follow them!'" (Revelation 14:13).

But regarding activity it also says, "No longer will there be a curse upon anything. For the throne of God and of the Lamb will be there, and his servants will worship him" (Revelation 22:3). Servants are active—they have things to do, places to go, people to see. We will be able to work as God intended, no longer under the Curse that can make work tedious and frustrating. Don't you love the idea of getting lots of rest *and* having plenty to do?

When we live our present lives in anticipation of our eternal resurrected lives, we will live differently. One day, money will be useless. While it's still useful, here and now, Christians with foresight will use it for the kind of good we will forever celebrate on the New Earth, our true and eternal home.

CHAPTER 11

God's Steward's Eternal Rewards

MANAGING GOD'S MONEY WELL requires a lifetime of daily decisions and actions. But we will only be motivated to make those decisions and take those actions if we are convinced that they really matter. If they *don't* matter to God, and if they *won't* matter for eternity, why should we bother to be faithful stewards in the first place? Why go to all that work of asking God what he wants us to do with his money and seeking to carefully and thoughtfully manage God's assets if in the end it really won't make any difference whether we managed them well or poorly?

The doctrine of eternal rewards is critical to the thinking of God's faithful stewards.

Does God care about what we *do* on Earth, or only about what we *believe*?

Scripture repeatedly states that all people, not just unbelievers, will be judged for their works, both good and bad. The Old Testament warns, "Don't excuse yourself by saying, 'Look, we didn't know.' For God understands all hearts, and he sees you. He who guards your soul knows you knew. He will repay all people as their actions deserve" (Proverbs 24:12). The New Testament echoes, "For we must all stand before Christ to be judged. We will each receive whatever we deserve for the good or evil we have done in this earthly body" (2 Corinthians 5:10).

All believers in Christ will give an account of their lives to their Lord. The result of this will be the gain or loss of eternal rewards.

God's Word treats this judgment with great sobriety. Our works are what we have done with our resources— time, energy, talents, money, possessions. The fire of God's holiness will reveal the quality of these works, the eternal significance of what we've done with our God-given assets and opportunities.

Paul describes the process of "building" our lives like constructing a physical building. For believers, our foundation is Christ, but all of us build with various materials—and we will be judged based on how we built: "Anyone who builds on that foundation may use a variety of materials—gold, silver, jewels, wood, hay, or straw. But on the judgment day, fire will reveal what kind of work each builder has done. The fire will show if a person's work has any value. If the work survives, that builder will receive a reward. But if the work is burned up, the builder will suffer great loss. The builder will be saved, but like someone barely escaping through a wall of flames" (1 Corinthians 3:12-15).

God is *for* his children, not against them (Romans 8:31). He wants to commend us at the judgment seat of Christ. He doesn't want the works of our lifetimes to go up in smoke. "By his divine power, God has given us everything we need for living a godly life" (2 Peter 1:3).

For those who have served Christ faithfully, the judgment seat will primarily be a time of commendation and celebration. He will reward us for acts of love that no one else even noticed. God "will not forget how hard you have worked for him and how you have shown your love to him by caring for other believers, as you still do" (Hebrews 6:10).

Does God hate our good works?

Sadly, many Christians have come to think of *works* as a dirty word. It isn't! Yes, God condemns works done to earn salvation and works done to impress others. But our Lord enthusiastically *commends* good works done for the right reasons. James writes, "Faith by itself isn't enough. Unless it produces good deeds, it is dead and useless. . . . If you are wise and understand God's ways, prove it by living an honorable life, doing good works with the humility that comes from wisdom" (James 2:17; 3:13).

God so values our good works—including good things for us to do with his money—that he says he created us in order to *do* good works! "It is by grace you have been saved, through faith—and this not from yourselves, it is the gift of God—not by works, so that no one can boast. For we are God's workmanship, *created in Christ Jesus to do good works, which God prepared in advance for us to do*" (Ephesians 2:8-10, NIV).

God entrusts to us time, gifting, opportunity, money, and possessions as resources to do these good works he has prepared for us to do. He will reward us according to whether or not we do them and the condition of our hearts as we do them.

We know Christ will say to some (but clearly not all) believers, "Well done, my good and faithful servant" (Matthew 25:21). Not "Well said," or "Well believed," but "Well *done*." What separates the sheep from the goats is what they did and didn't *do* with their God-entrusted resources of time, money, and possessions. Where we spend eternity, whether Heaven or Hell, depends on our *faith*. But how real that faith is will be demonstrated by our *works*.

How powerful is the motivation of eternal reward?

Receiving reward from Christ means unspeakable eternal gain. Forfeiting reward is a terrible loss with equally eternal implications. How dare we say that being in Heaven is all that matters to us, when God tells us so much else matters to him?

Once in Heaven, you and I will not have a second chance to move the hand of God through prayer to heal a hurting soul, share Christ with one who can be saved from Hell, care for the sick, give a cup of water to the thirsty, comfort the dying, invest money to aid the helpless, rescue the unborn, further God's Kingdom, open our homes, and share our clothes and food with the poor and needy.

If we really believed that what we do with our money and possessions—and everything else—will have an irreversible effect on eternity, wouldn't we live differently? Scripture does not teach what most of us seem to assume—that Heaven will transform each of us into equal beings with equal possessions, equal responsibilities, and equal capacities.

Is it wrong to be motivated by rewards?

The doctrine of God granting people eternal rewards for faithful obedience is the neglected key to unlocking our motivation. With long-term reward as his incentive, Moses chose short-term suffering: "He thought it was better to suffer for the sake of Christ than to own the treasures of Egypt, for he was looking ahead to his great reward" (Hebrews 11:26).

Paul ran his life's race with his eyes on the prize, which motivated him to run hard and long. He strove not to get a crown of laurel leaves that would rot but "to get a crown that will last forever" (1 Corinthians 9:25, NIV). Paul encouraged all believers to be motivated by rewards, saying, "Let's not get tired of doing what is good. At just the right time we will reap a harvest of blessing if we don't give up. Therefore, whenever we have the opportunity, we should do good to everyone—especially to those in the family of faith" (Galatians 6:9-10).

The greatest model of motivation by reward is Christ himself. He endured the cross "because of the joy awaiting him" (Hebrews 12:2). He humbled himself, knowing that he would ultimately be exalted (Philippians 2:9).

If we maintain that it's wrong to be motivated by rewards, we bring a serious accusation against Christ! First, because Scripture reveals that Jesus himself was motivated partly by the rewards that awaited him. And second, because we imply that our Lord is tempting us to sin every time he offers us rewards for obedience! Because God does not tempt his children, it's clear that whatever he lays before us as a motivation can only be legitimate.

Businesspeople work in a world of incentives. So do homemakers, schoolchildren, and all other human beings, regardless of age, nationality, or wealth. Every effective manager and every wise leader knows the importance of incentives. These are motivators that may be personal, social, spiritual, physical, or financial. Unfortunately, countless Christians consider incentives to be "secular," "carnal," or "unspiritual."

Most of us use rewards to motivate our children. So why are we surprised that God uses rewards to motivate us? By God's own design, *all* of us need incentives to motivate us to do our jobs and do them well.

Motivation by reward is not a result of the Fall; rather, it is God's original design for humanity. (Of course, like all things God created, it can be twisted and misused by sinful people.)

To say, "I don't do anything for the reward—I do it only because it's right," may appear to take the spiritual high ground. But, in fact, it's pseudospiritual. Saying that there's only one good reason to do something denies the other ways God himself uses to motivate us. It contradicts all the passages of Scripture that unmistakably attempt to motivate us by our desire for rewards.

Whose idea is it for God to grant rewards to faithful stewards?

Suppose years ago, when my daughters were teenagers, I told them, "If you put in a full day of yard work Saturday, I'll pay you sixty dollars and take you out to a nice dinner." Would they be wrong to *want* to receive that sixty dollars? Would they be wrong to look forward to going out to a nice dinner with their dad? Of course not! I'm their father, I made the offer, and I *want* them to desire those rewards!

Now, it would be inappropriate if my daughters refused to work unless and until I offered them rewards. But that's not the case—*rewarding them was my idea, not theirs.* In fact, my own joy would be lessened if they *didn't* want the rewards I offered them—particularly that special dinner together.

"But God doesn't owe us anything," people argue. "He has the right to expect us to work for him with no thought of reward." True, we should be willing and happy to serve him even without compensation. Jesus addresses this when he says, "So you also, when you have done everything you were told to do, should say, 'We are unworthy servants; we have only done our duty'" (Luke 17:10, NIV).

But what turns this debate on its head is one simple fact—it wasn't *our* idea that God reward us. It was *his* idea! Satan or the world didn't make it up. *God* thought of it. He designed us to need and want incentives to motivate us to do our jobs and do them well. How dare we minimize them and say, in essence, "I don't care about what God cared enough to offer me"?

Suppose one daughter did that day of yard work joylessly and then said, "Dad, I refuse to let you pay me, and I don't want to go to dinner with you." *How would that make me feel?* Refusing the reward I *want* to give her would not be honoring to me.

We flatter ourselves—and insult God—when we say, "I don't care about reward." The point is that *God* cares, and therefore so should we.

God *will* reward the child who gave to the missions offering the money she'd saved for a softball mitt. He'll reward the teenager who kept himself pure despite all the temptations. He'll reward the man who tenderly cared for his wife with Alzheimer's, the mother who raised the child with cerebral palsy, the child who rejoiced despite his handicap. He'll reward the unskilled person who was faithful and the skilled person who was meek and servant-hearted.

God will reward the parents who modeled Christ to their children, and he'll reward the children who followed him despite their parents' bad example. He'll reward those who suffered while trusting him, and those who helped the ones who were suffering. He'll reward the couple who sold their large house to live in a small one and gave the remaining money away to missions.

This isn't speculation, because Jesus clearly teaches that he rewards our good works: "Love your enemies! Do good to them. Lend to them without expecting to be repaid. Then your reward from heaven will be very great, and you will truly be acting as children of the Most High, for he is kind to those who are unthankful and wicked. . . . Invite the poor, the crippled, the lame, and the blind. Then at the resurrection of the righteous, God will reward you for inviting those who could not repay you" (Luke 6:35; 14:13-14).

God's money managers should desire his approval and look forward to his reward for their faithful service. Yet I have found for the last twenty-five years that there is a profound resistance to this doctrine among many Christians. They consider it "unspiritual" regardless of the fact that it is emphatically biblical! So let me repeat myself: God doesn't *have* to reward anyone for anything. He does it because he *wants* to. And make no mistake: That's exactly what he's going to do. "For the Son of Man is going to come in his Father's glory with his angels, and then he will reward each person *according to what he has done*" (Matthew 16:27, NIV).

Why does God reward people? Because he is pleased by what they've done. A child who wants to be rewarded by his parents realizes they will be pleased by his good deeds, and he delights in this. The child's desire for his father's approval is not mercenary. Rather it flows out of his love for him. Every father wants his children to desire his approval. And God chooses to show his approval through giving his children eternal rewards.

Should reward be our only motivation?

The Bible calls upon us to obey God out of several motivations. First, we should obey out of our *love* for him as Father and Redeemer: "Understand, therefore, that the LORD your God is indeed God. He is the faithful God who keeps his covenant for a thousand generations and lavishes his unfailing love on those who love him and obey his commands" (Deuteronomy 7:9).

Second, the Bible calls upon us to obey out of our *fear* of him as Creator and Judge: "Since we are receiving a Kingdom that is unshakable, let us be thankful and please God by worshiping him with holy fear and awe" (Hebrews 12:28).

Third, we obey out of our *hope* in him as rewarder of those who serve him: "It is impossible to please God without faith. Anyone who wants to come to him must believe that God exists and that he rewards those who sincerely seek him" (Hebrews 11:6).

Each of these motivations is legitimate, and each complements the other. So of course reward should never be our *only* motivation. But it is nonetheless a biblical and important motivation. Ultimately, "whether we are here in this body or away from this body, our goal is to please him" (2 Corinthians 5:9). Pleasing the one you love is its own lofty reward.

We must realize, once and for all, what Satan doesn't want us to understand—that it is emphatically biblical and appropriate for God's faithful stewards to look forward to his rewards. It is *not* anti-Christian. What is anti-Christian is the self-centeredness that's unconcerned about God and our neighbor, and the preoccupation with immediate fulfillment of desires that distracts us from finding our ultimate fulfillment in Christ.

Giving and Sharing God's Money and Possessions

CHAPTER 12

Tithing: The Training Wheels of Giving

Where and how do we start giving?

I have mixed feelings about the subject of tithing. I've had long discussions with fellow believers who view tithing in ways I don't think are biblical.

Some believe that tithing is the pinnacle of giving. They imagine that as long as we tithe, we have fulfilled our obligation to God and can do whatever we please with the remaining 90 percent (which supposedly belongs to us).

Others are utterly convinced—and have dedicated their lives to convincing others—that tithing should never be practiced under the New Covenant. They believe that anyone who thinks he should give a minimum of 10 percent to God is in bondage to legalism. They consider the teaching of tithing, and often the practice of it, to be a cancer in churches, a manipulative tool unscrupulous leaders use to fund their pet projects and exorbitant lifestyles. (Of course, there *are* such leaders, but the problem is with them, not with tithing.)

I am sometimes bewildered by these extremes, and I do not align myself with either of them. I address tithing here not to promote legalism, and not because I don't distinguish between the Old and New Covenants. I do it simply to begin where God began with his own children.

New Testament giving goes far beyond tithing (something that people holding both extreme positions fail to recognize). However, the principle of tithing was ingrained in the beliefs and lifestyles of the early Christians, most of whom grew up in Jewish homes.

There are many passages that teach the giving of the firstfruits and tithing (e.g., Exodus 22:29; Numbers 18:12, 24; Nehemiah 13:12). The firstfruits referred to the first products of the seasonal harvest. They were considered to be holy, God's sole possession. Symbolically, the giving of the firstfruits acknowledged God's ownership of the land and of all of the crops that would follow. Before people consumed any of the harvest, they were to give God the best representatives of the first part of that harvest. If this wasn't done, there would be no blessing on the remainder of the crop (Leviticus 19:23-25; 23:14; Deuteronomy 26:1-15; Proverbs 3:9-10).

While "firstfruits" doesn't indicate a specific proportion, tithing does. The first teaching about tithing as a law occurs in Leviticus 27:30: "A tithe of everything from the land, whether grain from the soil or fruit from the trees, belongs to the LORD; it is holy to the LORD" (NIV).

The tithe "belongs to the Lord," not to the one who pays it. The tithe applies to "everything," not just some things. It is "holy," to be set apart and given to God, not used for any other purpose.

Some argue that only farmers and herdsmen were expected to tithe. Were that true, in Israel's economy that would have been a very high percentage of the population. But there's every reason to believe that *everyone* earning an income was expected to give 10 percent. After all, why should non-farmers and non-herdsmen be exempt from a law that affirmed God's ownership, recognized his provision, and assisted spiritual governance of all citizens? Priests made offerings on behalf of all the people, not just farmers and herdsmen.

We're told, "The people of Israel gave in abundance the firstfruits of grain, wine, oil, honey, and of all the produce of the field. *And they brought in abundantly the tithe of everything*" (2 Chronicles 31:5, ESV). God doesn't speak here of just "the farmers of Israel" tithing, but "the people of Israel." The term is all encompassing, suggesting no exceptions.

The products mentioned in 2 Chronicles 31:5 are only examples. Then we're told "they [the people of Israel] brought in abundantly the tithe of *everything*." The term *everything* is all inclusive. If someone made and sold clothing or pottery or jewelry, surely the same level of devotion to God—as evidenced by the tithe—would be expected of him just as it was expected of farmers and herdsmen.

In the Bible's first reference to tithing, we're told of Melchizedek, "Abram gave him a tenth of everything" (Genesis 14:20, NIV). The "everything" referred to all the spoils of battle, which would have included precious jewels, pottery, clothing, art, eating utensils, and crafts, as well as money.

What exactly does tithing mean?

The meaning of the word *tithe* is "a tenth part." Some people use tithing as a synonym for giving, but it isn't. You can *donate* 2 percent or 4 percent or 6 percent of your income, but you cannot *tithe* it any more than you can "whitewash" a wall with red paint.

The Creator warned the Israelites that to present anything less than the full 10 percent was to "rob God," since the first 10 percent *belonged* to him, not them. The prophet Malachi warned the people against this attitude: "Should people cheat God? Yet you have cheated me! But you ask, 'What do you mean? When did we ever cheat you?' You have cheated me of the tithes and offerings due to me. You are under a curse, for your whole nation has been cheating me" (Malachi 3:8-9).

Notice that in addition to the tithe, God speaks of his people cheating him of "offerings due to me." Clearly their Lord had expectations of his people's giving above and beyond the tithe. Since a voluntary offering could be "due" God under the Old Covenant because he had desires and expectations regarding the giving of his individual children, why shouldn't we expect the same under the New Covenant? Of course, we don't know the exact amount he expects people to give in freewill offering—each individual must ask him for direction. But the point is that *God does have such expectations* and is not pleased when they aren't fulfilled.

In his law, God taught his people to set aside a tenth of their crops as a teaching tool: "You must set aside a tithe of your crops—one-tenth of all the crops you harvest each year. Bring this tithe to the designated place of worship—the place the LORD your God chooses for his name to be honored—and eat it there in his presence. This applies to your tithes of grain, new wine, olive oil, and the firstborn males of your flocks and herds. Doing this will teach you always to fear the LORD your God" (Deuteronomy 14:22-23).

By giving away 10 percent, they made a statement about the remaining 90 percent—it also belonged to their Creator.

Of course, like any good practice, *tithing can be misunderstood and abused*. But God intended it to give perspective when properly practiced. It reminded his people that everything comes from him. Whatever amount we choose to give should not be like a tip tossed mindlessly on a table after a meal. It should be a meaningful expression of our dependence upon God and gratitude to him.

Even if you don't believe there is a biblical argument for Christians beginning with the tithe, please don't dismiss the logical and practical benefits. For example, tithing is clear and consistent, and it can easily be taught, including to children. It increases the believer's sense of commitment to God's work.

Tithing can also be a significant factor in spiritual

growth. I just reread ten letters written to me by church families whose spiritual lives were revolutionized as they discovered how to give. Though a number of them now give significantly more than the tithe, seven of the ten specifically mention that, for them, raising their giving to the level of 10 percent was a defining spiritual breakthrough in their lives. They didn't *stop* with tithing, but that's how they got *started* in the discipline and joy of giving.

If Western Christians all gave a minimum of 10 percent, the goal of world evangelism and feeding the hungry would be within reach. But that would just be the beginning, because often people who learn to tithe move on to freewill offerings far beyond that.

Without a reference point, where do you start giving? Why not start where God started his children, Israel? Tithing may begin as a duty but often it becomes a delight. For faithful Israelites, unclenching their fists and opening them to God had a thousand trickle-down benefits. Is it really any different for us today?

Isn't tithing legalism?

I've heard many Christians argue—sometimes angrily—that tithing is legalism. They claim tithing is bondage and God's people have been liberated to practice only "grace giving."

Of course, tithing *is* legalistic and self-righteous for some people. So are church attendance, Bible reading, and prayer, as well as habits of dress, eating, drinking, and recreation. There's nothing in life that can't be corrupted by legalism. But the solution is not to stop going to church, praying, or reading Scripture. Neither is it to conclude that tithing is *inherently* legalistic. That's neither charitable nor credible, given the many Christians who quietly practice it in faith and have drawn closer to God as they've done so.

To understand this issue, we should better understand the Old Testament practice of tithing. The Israelites actually gave three different tithes, but one of those was given every third year, so that cumulatively the three tithes amounted to 23 percent of their income (Numbers 18:21, 24; Deuteronomy 12:17-18; 14:22-23, 28-29; 26:12-13).

But let's consider just one of these tithes, the one that supported the religious leaders, something that believers are told to do in the church era: "Those who are taught the word of God should provide for their teachers, sharing all good things with them" (Galatians 6:6). In contrast to the 10 percent the Israelites were commanded to give to the Levites for their spiritual leadership, the average giving of American Christians to support their churches, spiritual leaders, missions work, and the needy totals about 2.5 percent, one-fourth of a tithe. This statistic suggests that the Israelites were four times more responsive to the law of Moses than the average American Christian is to the grace of Christ! (Reread that last sentence and ask yourself if something needs to change.)

When you consider that many Old Testament saints

gave not just the other two tithes but freewill offerings above and beyond them, the gap between their giving and that of Christians today is truly stunning.

The "I only believe in grace giving" claim rings hollow if it suggests that God actually expects less of New Covenant Christians than Old Covenant people, and less of today's wealthy church members than yesterday's poor Israelites.

It seems to me that those making this claim need to reevaluate their concept of "grace giving." It's an insult to apply the term *grace* to this radical lowering of standards. When you consider that New Testament believers understand the redemptive work of Christ and have the indwelling Spirit of God, the irony becomes even sharper.

And consider the example of the early church, Spirit indwelled but certainly not wealthy: "All the believers were united in heart and mind. And they felt that what they owned was not their own, so they shared everything they had. The apostles testified powerfully to the resurrection of the Lord Jesus, and God's great blessing was upon them all. There were no needy people among them, because those who owned land or houses would sell them and bring the money to the apostles to give to those in need" (Acts 4:32-35).

Rather than falling short of tithing, the early Christians, faced with others' needs, went far beyond it: "They shared everything they had." They believed that "what they owned was not their own." It belonged to God, so they made it freely available.

Of course, we should be pro-grace and anti-legalism. But shouldn't we also be in favor of spiritual disciplines that can launch people into a life of consistent obedience? Countless people were launched into generous giving through starting with the tithe.

I'm sure there are many sincere and generous people who argue against tithing. However, after twenty-five years of hearing people speak against tithing, *I've found that most of these people use their arguments to excuse their* own *lack of generous giving.* And some take the moral high ground as they do it, thinking they are "living by grace," while they condemn those who see value in tithing as being "in bondage to law."

Those who say, "Tithing isn't for today," need to examine their hearts. Are they actually demeaning the transforming power of grace and advocating spiritual-sounding "grace giving" as a license to cling to material wealth? New Testament Christians model lives transformed by the radical grace of Christ—making them *more* sacrificial and generous, not less!

I view tithing as a child's first steps—*not* the best she'll ever do, but simply a good beginning, one which her parents celebrate. Tithing is like the training wheels on the bicycle of giving. If you don't need the training wheels, great. If you're giving away 20, 50, or 80 percent of your income, you don't need to think about tithing!

But sometimes the bicycle is just lying there, going nowhere, as in the cases of 40 percent of professing Christians who (surveys show) give away *nothing*. So instead of rejecting tithing out of hand, why not *try* the training wheels to help you learn a new discipline until you no longer need them? There is nothing to lose and a great deal to gain. (And if 10 percent seems legalistic to you, feel free to start at 11, 12, or 15!)

If tithing is no longer a law, could it still be a good idea?

Jesus affirmed that people should tithe, but he skewered the religious leaders who used tithing as an excuse to avoid other responsibilities: "What sorrow awaits you teachers of religious law and you Pharisees. Hypocrites! For you are careful to tithe even the tiniest income from your herb gardens, but you ignore the more important aspects of the law—justice, mercy, and faith. You should tithe, yes, but do not neglect the more important things" (Matthew 23:23).

Because Jesus directly affirmed it in this passage ("you should tithe"), and prominent church fathers such as Augustine, Jerome, and Irenaeus taught it as a Christian norm, it seems to me the burden of proof falls on those who say tithing is *not* a minimum standard for God's people.

Some argue against tithing by saying, "The New Testament advocates voluntary offerings." Yes, of course it does, but as we've seen, so does the Old Testament. Voluntary giving is not a new concept. Having a minimum standard of giving has never been incompatible with giving above and beyond that standard. It's not a matter of *either* the minimum of tithing *or* the above and beyond of voluntary offering. The two can easily coexist, as they have in our family for decades.

It isn't that the "floor" of the tithe is made invalid under the New Covenant but simply that the "ceiling" of Christian giving goes far above it. When Jesus told the disciples to go the second mile, he assumed they had already gone the first.

Tithing isn't the finish line of giving; it's the starting block. But, apparently, many of us need help getting started!

For many years wearing a seat belt wasn't a legal requirement. But even then, it was still a good idea. Suppose the seat-belt law were repealed. Would I stop wearing mine? Would I tell my children or grand-children, "Take off your seat belts. We're not under the law, and we're not going to be legalistic, so no more seat belts for us"? Of course not. A good idea is a good idea, whether or not it's the law.

If you have learned the discipline of radical giving out of a heart transformed by Christ's grace and you have no need to start with tithing, good for you. But don't conclude that other Christians, whether children or adults, can't benefit from using the tithe as a helpful guideline to jump-start a life of Christ-centered giving.

What if we can't afford to tithe?

When people tell me, "I can't afford to tithe," I often ask, "If your income were reduced by 10 percent, would you die?" They always admit they wouldn't. Somehow, they would manage to get by. That's proof that they really can tithe. The truth is simply that they don't *want* to.

In recent times of economic difficulty, countless people have been living on 10, 20, and 50 percent less than they used to. It isn't easy, but most manage to make it (proving they were wrong if they believed they couldn't live on 10 percent less).

Ironically, many people "can't afford" to give, precisely because they're not giving. If the minimum of tithing were expected by God and he promised to provide for those who trusted and obeyed him, doesn't it seem reasonable to expect that today he would empower me to get by on 90 percent instead of 100 percent? In fact, aren't I a lot safer living on less inside God's will than living on more outside it?

It comes down to priorities. The Israelites who had returned to their homeland from exile found themselves in a similar dilemma. They busily spent all their money and time working on their farms and building their homes, but they let God's house, his Temple, lie in ruins. Clearly this was a case of mismanaged priorities, so God spoke through his prophet Haggai: "You hoped for rich harvests, but they were poor. And when you brought your harvest home, I blew it away. Why? Because my house lies in ruins, says the LORD of Heaven's Armies, while all of you are busy building your own fine houses" (Haggai 1:9).

God wants us to get our priorities in line with his.

To do this, he often takes money we should have given him and blows it away! When we withhold giving, instead of blessing our financial transactions, he often puts them under a curse.

Many Christians testify that they live just as easily on the 90 percent (and others on the 70 or 80) as the 100 percent. People have told me that their financial problems began not when they tithed but when they withheld the tithe. I'll never forget a couple telling me they had experienced great joy when they had practiced tithing for several years, gradually increasing their giving beyond it, only to be told in their next Bible-teaching church that tithing was legalism. They began "grace giving," which, as they understood it, meant God no longer expected them to stretch themselves in their giving. Consequently their giving shrank and shrank, and so did their faith and spiritual vitality. Finally, they returned to their former practice of giving a minimum of 10 percent, which they found not burdensome but liberating and joyful.

I'm often asked, "If I haven't been giving at all, won't God understand if I move toward it gradually, starting at 3 percent or 5 percent?" Well, 3 or 5 percent is certainly better than nothing. But suppose I told you I've been robbing convenience stores, knocking off about a dozen a year. Then I say, "This year I'm only going to rob a half dozen!"

Well, granted, that's an improvement. But what would you advise me to do? *Surely the solution to robbing God is not to start robbing him less. It's to stop robbing him at all.*

Malachi 3 (NIV) calls it "robbing God" and "cheating" him, to give less than the tithe *and* to do less free-will giving than he desired them to. *Since New Testament Christians are called upon to give freewill offerings, surely it is also possible for us to rob God.* Do we rob him by giving him less than a tithe? Or by withholding freewill offerings he desires from us? These are questions God's money managers need to ask and answer.

Should we tithe on our gross or our net income?

Gross is the total amount God provides; net is what is left after taxes and other deductions. Some say that money we don't see is not true income. But are we not the beneficiaries of taxes and insurance and other withholdings from our paychecks?

If God bases his blessing on what we give, then we should ask ourselves what we want to be blessed on—the gross or the net. Do we not desire, as Malachi 3:10 says, that God would open the windows of Heaven and pour out blessings? (And, by the way, shouldn't we trust him to choose what form those blessings should take, even if we do not see the financial prosperity we hope for?)

As we faithfully give to him, God frequently entrusts more to our care. May we continue to be generous and wise with whatever amount of his money the God of sovereign grace calls upon us to manage.

CHAPTER 13

Freewill Giving: Overflow of the Grace-Filled Heart

GIVING IS A form of grace. We love because God first loved us, and we give because he first gave to us. Giving isn't just God's way of raising money—it's his way of raising children.

To give is to be like Jesus, whose incarnation and atonement were the ultimate lavish gift. In a passage about financial giving to the needy, Paul says, "For you know the grace of our Lord Jesus Christ, that though he was rich, yet for your sakes he became poor, so that you through his poverty might become rich" (2 Corinthians 8:9, NIV). God's unfolding drama of redemption is the essence of giving, the source of giving, and the model for giving.

When the Israelites gave voluntary offerings for the building of God's Tabernacle, they gave so much that the workers had to ask them to stop! "Finally the craftsmen who were working on the sanctuary left their work. They went to Moses and reported, 'The people have given more than enough materials to complete the job the LORD has commanded us to do!' So Moses gave the command, and this message was sent throughout the camp: 'Men and women, don't prepare any more gifts for the sanctuary. We have enough!'" (Exodus 36:4-6).

How many of us have been part of such a contagious outpouring of generous giving?

Consider what happened when King David made preparations for his son Solomon to build God's Temple. David set the example of giving: "Because of my devotion to the Temple of my God, I am giving all of my own private treasures of gold and silver to help in the construction. This is in addition to the building materials I have already collected for his holy Temple" (1 Chronicles 29:3).

The king's example was gladly followed by leaders throughout the land: "The family leaders, the leaders of the tribes of Israel, the generals and captains of the army, and the king's administrative officers all gave willingly" (verse 6). In turn, others followed their example: "The people rejoiced over the offerings, for they had given freely and wholeheartedly to the LORD, and King David was filled with joy" (verse 9).

How does grace giving differ from tithing?

The voluntary offerings went beyond the tithe. They constituted true giving, because the tithe was more a debt repaid to God, not a gift *per se*.

God's children gave more, sometimes much more,

as needs and opportunities arose. If the tithe was a demonstration of obedience, then voluntary offerings were a demonstration of love, joy, and worship.

When a friend was trying to figure out how much he should give monthly, he decided to give at least as much as his house payment. He told me, "If I can't afford to give that much, then I can't afford to live in a house this nice." He didn't reason from the tithe, he reasoned from his house payment, which was significantly greater than 10 percent.

Though God desired his people to do it joyfully, tithing required no heart response. But the freewill offering was different. It involved the joy of a heart touched by God's grace.

I object to the widespread notion that God's people, Israel, labored under a dreary legalism in their giving. On the contrary, the Old Testament emphasizes "freewill offerings" or "voluntary offerings." These were included along with the required tithes: "Bring your burnt offerings, your sacrifices, your tithes, your sacred offerings, your offerings to fulfill a vow, your voluntary offerings . . ." (Deuteronomy 12:6). The Israelites got caught up in the thrill of giving, as exhibited in their joyful contributions toward the building of the Tabernacle: "The people of Israel—every man and woman who was eager to help in the work the LORD had given them through Moses—brought their gifts and gave them freely to the LORD" (Exodus 35:29).

Here we see that Old Testament giving went far beyond tithing. The emphasis is not on the amount of the offering but on the willingness of each person's heart. It wasn't a tithe, which was obligatory; instead, it was given "freely."

Ironically, Christians who consider tithing the pinnacle or high ground of giving are actually lowering the Old Testament standard, which merely *started* with the tithe (or one of the tithes) but did not end there. Should the church, transformed by the redemptive work of Christ, experience such passionate giving *less* than our Israelite counterparts? Or should we experience it all the *more*?

God's gift to us is the lightning; our giving to him is the thunder. As lightning precedes thunder, so God's grace both precedes and causes our giving. This is clearly evident in 2 Corinthians 8–9, a passage that addresses giving as a response to God's grace and in response to the great needs of others.

Giving involves money, but much more. We can give a meal, a house, a dress, a shovel, a bicycle, a sewing machine, or any other possession. Or we can *share* any possession freely while still maintaining ownership. I know many people who are very generous with their possessions, quick to serve others with no strings attached. They loan their books, cars, camping equipment, or laptop computers. I'm convinced God will reward them not just for giving but for sharing.

Two cautions are in order. First, we can easily rationalize owning unnecessary things on the grounds that we share them with others. The fact that we can share doesn't mean it's the wisest or most strategic purchase.

We must also guard against possessiveness. If we're the kind of people that others are afraid to borrow from because they know that a dent or scratch or break would bother us, we're not having much of a ministry no matter how "willing to share" we imagine ourselves to be.

What do we do with the financial blessings God showers on us in response to our giving?

Jesus said, "Give, and you will receive. Your gift will return to you in full—pressed down, shaken together to make room for more, running over, and poured into your lap. The amount you give will determine the amount you get back" (Luke 6:38).

R. G. LeTourneau, an inventor of earthmoving machines, gave away 90 percent of his income to the Lord. As he put it, "I shovel out the money, and God shovels it back—but God has a bigger shovel." He lived the proverb: "Give freely and become more wealthy; be stingy and lose everything. The generous will prosper; those who refresh others will themselves be refreshed" (Proverbs 11:24-25).

My family has experienced God's "bigger shovel," his abundant material provision to the giver. In some cases it's obvious—such as an unexpected check in the mail or being given something just when we thought we'd have to buy it. One time we discovered an error we had made in our bank balance, finding we had more money than we realized.

In other cases, God's provision is less obvious but equally real. A washing machine that should have stopped a decade ago keeps on working. A car with two hundred thousand miles on it runs for two years without so much as a tune-up. A checking account that should have dried up long before the end of the month somehow makes it through. As God miraculously stretched the widow's oil supply in Elisha's day (2 Kings 4:1-7), and as he made the Israelites' clothes and sandals last forty years in the wilderness (Deuteronomy 8:4), I'm convinced he sometimes graciously extends the life of things that would normally have to be replaced.

Why has God provided more than we need?

Whether or not you're a giver, you have considerable material blessings from God. Have you ever asked yourself, "*Why* has he provided so much?" You don't need to wonder. God tells us *exactly* why: "God is the one who provides seed for the farmer and then bread to eat. In the same way, he will provide and increase your resources and then produce a great harvest of generosity in you. Yes, *you will be enriched [made rich] in every way so that . . .*" (2 Corinthians 9:10-11).

So that *what*? How *you* finish the sentence determines your stewardship future. Prosperity theology would finish it like this: ". . . so that we might live in wealth, showing the world how much God blesses those who love him."

But that isn't how Paul completes the sentence. He

says, "You will be made rich in every way *so that you can always be generous.*"

When God provides excess income, we often suppose, "This is a blessing." Yes, but it would be just as biblical to think, *This is a test.* Abundance isn't God's provision for me to live in luxury. It's his provision for me to help others live. God entrusts me with his money not to build my kingdom on Earth but to build his Kingdom in Heaven. When thinking clearly, I will see that often he wants me to downsize my temporary kingdom in order to upsize his eternal Kingdom.

Part of that process is not only to give but to give *cheerfully.* "Remember this—a farmer who plants only a few seeds will get a small crop. But the one who plants generously will get a generous crop. You must each decide in your heart how much to give. And don't give reluctantly or in response to pressure. 'For God loves a person who gives cheerfully.' And God will generously provide all you need. Then you will always have everything you need and plenty left over to share with others" (2 Corinthians 9:6-8).

It doesn't get much clearer than that!

Paul explained in the previous chapter: "At the present time your plenty will supply what they need, so that in turn their plenty will supply what you need. Then there will be equality, as it is written: 'He who gathered much did not have too much, and he who gathered little did not have too little'" (2 Corinthians 8:14-15, NIV).

Why does God give some of his children more than

they need and others less than they need? So that he may use his children to help one another. When those with too much give to those with too little, two problems are solved. When they don't, two problems are perpetuated.

Too often we assume that God entrusts more to us to increase our standard of living, yet his stated purpose is to increase our standard of giving.

How do we set our own salaries?

The Owner, God, has put each of our names on his account. We have unrestricted access to it, a privilege that is subject to abuse.

As his money managers, God trusts us to set our own salaries. We draw needed funds from his wealth to pay our living expenses. One of our central spiritual decisions is determining an amount that is reasonable to live on. Whatever that amount is—and it will legitimately vary from person to person—we shouldn't hoard or waste the excess. After all, it's his, not ours. And he has something to say about where to put it.

The money manager has legitimate needs, and the Owner is generous. He doesn't demand that his stewards live in poverty, and he doesn't resent us for making reasonable expenditures on ourselves. But suppose the Owner sees us living luxuriously in a mansion, driving only the best cars, and flying first class. Isn't there a point where, as stewards, we can cross the line of reasonable expenses?

Suppose you have something important you want delivered to someone who needs it. You wrap it up and hand it over to the FedEx delivery person. What would you think if, instead of delivering the package, the driver took it home, opened it, and kept it?

Imagine confronting him and hearing him say, "If you didn't want me to keep it, why'd you give it to me in the first place?"

You'd respond, "You don't get it. The package doesn't belong to you. You're just the middleman. Your job is to get the package from me and deliver it to those I want to have it."

We need to stop thinking of ourselves as owners and instead see ourselves as God's couriers. Just because God puts his money in our hands doesn't mean he intends for it to stay there!

Whose praise do we seek in giving?

Generous giving isn't meant to become a badge, something done for recognition or feeding pride. An incident in the early church makes this painfully clear. A man named Barnabas sold a field and brought all the money to the apostles for the church to use. Perhaps he was praised for it. In any case, Ananias and Sapphira also sold a piece of property. They decided to keep some of the money for themselves. That was their right, but when they brought the money to the apostles, they claimed it to be the entire amount of the sale. Presumably they were hoping to be praised. But they did not get what they hoped for:

> Now a man named Ananias, together
> with his wife Sapphira, also sold a piece of
> property. With his wife's full knowledge he
> kept back part of the money for himself, but
> brought the rest and put it at the apostles'
> feet. Then Peter said, "Ananias, how is it
> that Satan has so filled your heart that you
> have lied to the Holy Spirit and have kept
> for yourself some of the money you received
> for the land? Didn't it belong to you before
> it was sold? . . . You have not lied to men
> but to God." When Ananias heard this, he
> fell down and died. . . . Three hours later
> his wife came in, not knowing what had
> happened. Peter asked her, "Tell me, is this
> the price you and Ananias got for the land?"
> "Yes," she said, "that is the price." Peter said
> to her, "How could you agree to test the
> Spirit of the Lord? Look! The feet of the men
> who buried your husband are at the door,
> and they will carry you out also." . . .
> Then the young men came in and, finding
> her dead, carried her out and buried her
> beside her husband. (Acts 5:1-10, NIV)

If we are tempted to appear as if we're giving or sacrificing more than we are, we should take seriously what God did to Ananias and Sapphira. (This is not a club we want to join!)

What is sacrificial giving?

What does it mean to give beyond our ability? It means to push our giving past the point where the figures add up. It means to give away not just the luxuries but also some of the necessities. It means living with the faith of the poor widow Jesus commended to his disciples (Mark 12:41-44).

The Macedonian Christians were dirt poor, yet when they heard of needy people in Jerusalem, "they gave according to their means . . . and beyond their means, of their own accord, begging us earnestly for the favor of taking part in the relief of the saints" (2 Corinthians 8:3-4, ESV). When told they were too poor to give, they *begged* for the privilege of helping out! For most of us, giving *according* to our means would stretch us. Giving *beyond* our means would stretch us or even appear to break us. But it won't—because we know God is faithful.

Giving sacrificially also means giving the best. If we have two blankets and someone needs one of them, sacrificial giving hands over the better of the two. Sadly, much of our "giving" is merely discarding. Parting with something we didn't want in the first place isn't giving; it's selective disposal. When God commanded David to build an altar in a certain location, the owner of the land offered to give it to David. But David insisted on buying it, saying, "I will not sacrifice to the LORD my God burnt offerings that cost me nothing" (2 Samuel 24:24, NIV). When David gave, he intended to give sacrificially. He would not give merely his leftovers.

Sacrificial giving makes no human sense. But we are to think like Christ, not the world. Paul was a recipient of such sacrificial giving by the churches in Macedonia. He honored those givers, using them as an example as he wrote to the church in Corinth, "Out of the most severe trial, their overflowing joy and their extreme poverty welled up in rich generosity. For I testify that they gave as much as they were able, and even beyond their ability" (2 Corinthians 8:2-3, NIV).

A single man in our church came to Christ in his twenties, read the Scriptures, and got so excited that he decided to sell his house and give all the money to God. But when he shared this plan with older believers in his Bible study group, something tragic happened: They talked him out of it.

If we ever feel inclined to talk a young believer, including our own child, out of giving, we should restrain ourselves. Let's not quench God's Spirit and rob loved ones of the present joy and future rewards of giving. Instead, let's lay God's assets on the table and ask him which ones he wants *us* to give away.

We don't like risky faith. We like to have our safety net below us in case God fails to catch us. If we give at all, we will give as much as we can without really feeling it, and no more. We take away the high stakes, and we also lose the high returns. We miss the adventure of seeing God provide when we've really stretched ourselves.

God's money manager doesn't ask, "How much more can I keep?" but "How much more can I give?" Whenever we start to get comfortable with our level of giving, it's time to ask God if he wants us to raise it again.

CHAPTER 14

Helping the Poor and Spreading the Gospel: Supporting God's Work with God's Wealth

CARING FOR THE poor and helpless is so basic to the Christian faith that those who don't do it aren't considered true heaven-bound believers. Jesus' story about the "sheep" and the "goats" makes this clear. Don't skim this; read every word:

> All the nations will be gathered in his presence, and he will separate the people as a shepherd separates the sheep from the goats. He will place the sheep at his right hand and the goats at his left. Then the King will say to those on his right, "Come, you who are blessed by my Father, inherit the Kingdom prepared for you from the creation of the world. For I was hungry, and you fed me. I was thirsty, and you gave me a drink. I was a stranger, and you invited me into your home. I was naked,

and you gave me clothing. I was sick, and you cared for me. I was in prison, and you visited me." Then these righteous ones will reply, "Lord, when did we ever see you hungry and feed you? Or thirsty and give you something to drink? Or a stranger and show you hospitality? Or naked and give you clothing? When did we ever see you sick or in prison and visit you?" And the King will say, "I tell you the truth, when you did it to one of the least of these my brothers and sisters, you were doing it to me! Then the King will turn to those on the left and say, 'Away with you, you cursed ones, into the eternal fire prepared for the devil and his demons. For I was hungry, and you didn't feed me. I was thirsty, and you didn't give me a drink. I was a stranger, and you didn't invite me into your home. I was naked, and you didn't give me clothing. I was sick and in prison, and you didn't visit me.' Then they will reply, 'Lord, when did we ever see you hungry or thirsty or a stranger or naked or sick or in prison, and not help you?' And he will answer, 'I tell you the truth, when you refused to help the least of these my brothers and sisters, you were refusing to help me.' And they will go away into eternal punishment, but the righteous will go into eternal life." (Matthew 25:32-46)

Are we to blame for people's poverty?

Neither God's Word nor an accurate understanding of economics supports the notion that the prosperous are automatically responsible for making others poor. What Scripture does say is that even when we're not at fault, we are responsible to *help* the poor. "If you help the poor, you are lending to the LORD—and he will repay you!" (Proverbs 19:17).

Ignoring the poor is not an option for the godly. In the account of the final judgment, the sin held against the "goats" is not that they did something wrong to those in need but that they failed to do anything right for them. Theirs is a sin of *omission* with grave eternal consequences.

This means we cannot wash our hands of responsibility to the poor by saying, "I'm not doing anything to hurt them." We must actively be doing something to help them.

We should ask, "If Christ were on the other side of the street, or the city, or even the world, and he were hungry, thirsty, helpless, or imprisoned for his faith, would we help him?" But we mustn't forget what Christ himself says in Matthew 25: He *is* in our neighborhood, community, city, country, and across the world in the form of poor and needy people—and especially in those who are persecuted for their faith.

We're not to feel guilty that God has entrusted us with abundance. But we are to feel responsible to compassionately and wisely use that abundance to help the less fortunate. John Wesley wrote, "Put yourself in the place of every poor man and deal with him as you would have God deal with you."

Does how we help the poor depend on the reasons why they are poor?

The worst thing we can do to the poor is ignore them. The next worst thing is to help them only enough to keep them alive but not enough to assist them out of poverty.

Those we help should be needy, and those responsible to help them first are their family members. Paul explained this to Timothy: "Take care of any widow who has no one else to care for her. But if she has children or grandchildren, their first responsibility is to show godliness at home and repay their parents by taking care of them. This is something that pleases God" (1 Timothy 5:3-4).

The poor are frequently lumped together into one group as if they're all the same. But neither Scripture nor experience indicates that all poor people are poor for the same reasons. Consequently, they cannot all be truly helped by the same means.

If people are poor because their homes and businesses have been wiped out in a flood, the solution may be to give them money, materials, and assistance to rebuild their homes and reestablish their businesses. If they're poor because of insufficient natural resources or adverse climate, we can share the knowledge, skills, and technology necessary to help them make the best of their situation. If this is impossible, we might help them relocate. If people are poor due to oppression or injustice in our nation, then we can petition and lobby for legal, social, and economic reforms.

A person may be poor because of self-indulgence. "Those who love pleasure become poor" (Proverbs 21:17). Such a person needs only to liquidate his assets to feed his family, then learn to live within his means and not squander his income.

Some poverty is due to laziness (Proverbs 24:30-34). Ultimately, even though he doesn't want to be poor, the lazy man is poor by choice.

Lazy and self-indulgent people do not need financial support; they need incentives to no longer be lazy and self-indulgent. Acts of well-meaning provision can remove their incentive to be responsible for themselves. Paul explained this in no uncertain terms to the church in Thessalonica: "Even while we were with you, we gave you this command: 'Those unwilling to work will not get to eat.' Yet we hear that some of you are living idle lives, refusing to work and meddling in other people's business. We command such people and urge them in the name of the Lord Jesus Christ to settle down and work to earn their own living" (2 Thessalonians 3:10-12).

There's much to learn from the Old Testament practice of gleaning. This was God's way of helping to provide for the poor of the land (Leviticus 19:9-10).

The corners of the fields were left uncut so the poor could have food. But the grain wasn't cut, bundled, processed, ground, bagged, transported, and delivered to the poor. Provided they were able, the poor did the work themselves—and thereby were neither robbed of their dignity nor made irresponsible by a system requiring no work.

When in doubt, we should err on the side of helping the poor, even though we may have to swallow our pride and realize we've been misled. Martin Luther was so generous he was sometimes taken advantage of. In 1541, a transient woman, allegedly a runaway nun, came to their home. Martin and Katherine fed and housed her, only to discover she had lied and stolen. Yet Luther believed no one would become poor by practicing charity.

What's our heart condition as we give to the poor?

The prophet Isaiah spoke God's message to the people regarding their attitude toward the poor in their midst: "This is the kind of fasting I want: Free those who are wrongly imprisoned; lighten the burden of those who work for you. Let the oppressed go free, and remove the chains that bind people. Share your food with the hungry, and give shelter to the homeless. Give clothes to those who need them, and do not hide from relatives who need your help. Then your salvation will come like the dawn, and your wounds will quickly heal. Your godliness will lead you forward, and the glory of the LORD will protect you from behind" (Isaiah 58:6-8).

We need to examine our motives. It's becoming trendy for the middle and upper classes to help the poor. It causes people to feel good and soothes their consciences to make a few token gestures to the poor before returning to their materialism. The challenge is to integrate caring for the poor into our lifestyles.

Some seem to think that giving to a good cause is all that matters. But Paul says, "If I gave everything I have to the poor and even sacrificed my body, I could boast about it; but if I didn't love others, I would have gained nothing" (1 Corinthians 13:3).

What about giving to world evangelism?

Paul says that the gospel is "most important" (1 Corinthians 15:3). Given the crisis of the Hell-bent human condition, spreading the gospel is likewise "most important." Sadly, church budgets often designate less than 10 percent of their income to world missions. Americans spend more on chewing gum than on world missions.

Christ is glorified not simply by the total number who worship him but also by the fact that this number includes representatives from every tribe, language, people, and nation (Revelation 5:9; 7:9). Therefore, we must make concerted efforts to see that missionaries reach the "hidden" people who have not yet heard the gospel.

We are motivated first by the glory of God, but we're also moved by the eternal needs of people. Many decry the fact that some don't believe in Hell. But there's a shame even greater—that we who *do* believe in Hell make so little effort to keep others from going there.

Some people still debate whether it is more important to care for people's physical needs or their spiritual needs. This assumes a false dichotomy. Jesus commanded his followers both to take the gospel to the world and to feed, clothe, and care for the needy.

The dead do not hear the gospel; to allow people to die or suffer needlessly when we could prevent it is not what it means to be a Christ follower.

On the other hand, people who don't hear the gospel can't go to Heaven (Romans 10:13-14). Feeding them is right, but neglecting to share the gospel with people who will likely soon leave this world is wrong. We are to both live out the gospel *and* share the gospel.

Where should we give first?

In the early church, the new believers shared their belongings. Luke wrote, "There were no needy people among them, because those who owned land or houses would sell them and bring the money to the apostles to give to those in need" (Acts 4:34-35).

Note that the believers brought the money "to the apostles." They entrusted their gifts to spiritually qualified church leaders, who distributed them wisely.

Giving should start with your local Bible-believing, Christ-centered church, the spiritual community where you're fed and to which you're accountable. In the New Testament, giving was not directed to the church at large, the universal body of Christ, but to the local Christian assembly. Even gifts that were sent to other places were given *through* the local church.

Normally, I think firstfruits should go to the local church. But I don't believe in "storehouse tithing" if it means that a church hoards funds or spends them on frills or monuments to ego and prosperity. Freewill giving beyond the tithe also can go to worthy parachurch ministries. I believe that both types of ministry deserve support, but our giving should begin with our primary spiritual community.

Much unwise giving today stems from forgetting that we are giving money that belongs to God, not us. Sometimes the heart attitude, if spoken honestly, would sound like this: "I give *my* money to this place and that place as I see fit, rather than giving to the church to have it distributed as the spiritual leaders see fit. I enjoy receiving recognition and ego strokes from those I send my money to."

If believers entrusted the distribution of their God-given funds to qualified local church leaders (I realize that some church leaders aren't qualified), the worthy parachurch ministries would thrive and the unworthy ones would fade away.

What if we disagree with how the local church uses money?

God puts people in positions of leadership—in government, workplace, family, and church. Our attitude toward church leaders should be as commanded:

- "Everyone must submit to governing authorities. For all authority comes from God, and those in positions of authority have been placed there by God" (Romans 13:1).
- "Obey your spiritual leaders, and do what they say. Their work is to watch over your souls, and they are accountable to God. Give them reason to do this with joy and not with sorrow" (Hebrews 13:17).

Is it possible that your church leaders are in a better position to judge what to do with contributions than you are? If the Bible tells me to pay taxes (Romans 13:6) and I comply, even though some will be wasted and even used for bad purposes, surely I can give to God through my church even when I don't feel comfortable with every use of the funds.

Of course, if *God's* money is going to Bible-denying seminaries and groups that promote immorality, it's time to speak to my church leaders. If I still cannot in good conscience give regularly and substantially to my church, perhaps it's time to ask God for help finding a church where I can give as he has directed.

What should we look for when giving to a ministry?

Donors might ask the parachurch ministries they support whether they are paying to get celebrity endorsements or are spending their funds in some way other than it appears. If the answers aren't ethically and biblically satisfactory, donors should communicate that until changes occur, they can no longer support the ministry. Why? Because they are handling *God's* money, and as his stewards they must only invest it where God's ethical standards are followed and his name is honored.

To learn which characteristics to look for in a ministry you might choose to support, see my article "Nineteen Questions to Ask Before You Give to Any Organization," available on our ministry's Web site, www.epm.org/19questions.

Of course, no organization is perfect. But if you wait to give until you find the perfect ministry, you'll never give. And for the Christian transformed by the riches of God's grace, failing to give simply isn't an option.

Wisely Handling God's Money and Possessions

CHAPTER 15

Discipleship: Choosing a Strategic Lifestyle

SOME THINK WE should emulate Jesus' lifestyle: "Foxes have holes and birds of the air have nests, but the Son of Man has no place to lay his head" (Matthew 8:20, NIV).

Critics speak out in magazine articles, books, and sermons against today's materialistic Christians. Much of what they say is accurate, but they sometimes make faulty assumptions about the biblical texts.

There was a striking difference between the itinerant ministry of Jesus and the apostles as seen in the Gospels and the settled communities of Christians reflected in the later books of the New Testament.

Do Christ's followers have a right to own land and possessions?

Jesus called his first four disciples to leave their fishing business:

> One day as Jesus was walking along the shore of the Sea of Galilee, he saw Simon and his

brother Andrew throwing a net into the water,
for they fished for a living. Jesus called out to
them, "Come, follow me, and I will show you
how to fish for people!" And they left their
nets at once and followed him. A little farther
up the shore Jesus saw Zebedee's sons, James
and John, in a boat repairing their nets. He
called them at once, and they also followed
him, leaving their father, Zebedee, in the boat
with the hired men. (Mark 1:16-20)

Abandoning their possessions was part of answer-
ing the call because Christ's ministry was itinerant,
requiring regular travel on foot. To follow Christ, the
disciples simply *had* to leave their boats and nets. The
central point isn't that they left their boats but that they
followed Jesus.

But even these apostles didn't irreversibly divest
themselves of all possessions. In Mark 1:29, just ten
verses after they've left their nets, "they went to Simon
and Andrew's home." These disciples who left their
home to follow Jesus still had a home.

The Gospels repeatedly refer to Jesus and the disciples traveling by boat on the Sea of Galilee. Most
likely, the boat belonged to one of the fishermen-
turned-apostles.

Peter says to Jesus, "We have left everything to
follow you!" (Mark 10:28, NIV). He doesn't say, "We
have *sold* everything," though they may have liquidated
many of their possessions (Luke 12:32-33). When Jesus

entrusted his mother, Mary, to the care of John the apostle, John himself writes, "From that time on, this disciple took her into his home" (John 19:26-27, NIV). After three years of following Jesus, John still had a home, and Jesus' mother went to live with him there.

Levi the tax collector represents the kind of disciple who utilizes possessions for Kingdom causes rather than walking away from them. "Follow me," Jesus told him, and Levi got up and followed him (Mark 2:14). In the very next verse, a dinner party in Levi's house is used to introduce people to Jesus. Given his profession and the number of people at the party, Levi's house was undoubtedly nicer and larger than average. We're never told that Jesus called Levi to sell his house. Maybe he did; maybe he didn't.

Although large crowds followed Jesus, he chose only twelve apostles to join him in his itinerant ministry, traveling and preaching (Mark 3:13-19). Others from the crowd also followed Jesus. They weren't chosen as apostles but served as disciples. When they weren't with Jesus, where did these disciples go? Back to their families, homes, fields, livestock, and jobs. Just as for most of his life Jesus had served God working as a carpenter and living in a house on a piece of land, so most of his disciples served God as faithful stewards, raising their families and working in their own communities.

Clearly, the majority of Christ's followers never divested themselves of all their possessions, nor did he expect them to.

Should we go out, leaving possessions behind, or stay home and support others?

When Jesus chose the Twelve, he did so carefully, after much prayer. "Afterward Jesus went up on a mountain and called out the ones he wanted to go with him. And they came to him. Then he appointed twelve of them and called them his apostles. They were to accompany him, and he would send them out to preach, giving them authority to cast out demons" (Mark 3:13-15). Undoubtedly others would have been delighted to be chosen. They may have been disappointed at having to return to their houses and jobs to serve Christ in a "normal" life. But it was his choice, not theirs.

After Jesus healed him, the Gerasene demoniac wanted desperately to leave everything and follow Christ. "As Jesus was getting into the boat, the man who had been demon possessed begged to go with him" (Mark 5:18). The next verse is significant: "Jesus said, 'No, go home to your family, and tell them everything the Lord has done for you and how merciful he has been.'" Although Christ called some to *leave* their homes, he instructed this man to *go* to his home. Christ knew that God's Kingdom could be better served if this man made his home his base for serving God.

Was this an inferior calling? Judge by the results: "So the man started off to visit the Ten Towns of that region and began to proclaim the great things Jesus had done for him; and everyone was amazed" (verse 20). Christ called this transformed man to settle back in his own community, steward what possessions he had, and be a powerful witness there.

When Jesus sent his twelve disciples out two by two to minister in villages, he told them to take nothing for their journey except a walking stick—no food, no traveler's bag, no money. He allowed them to wear sandals but not to take a change of clothes. "'Wherever you go,' he said, 'stay in the same house until you leave town'" (Mark 6:10). Traveling missionaries take nothing except what facilitates their travels (in the case of the twelve disciples, this included only a staff, sandals, and the clothes on their backs). Others are "settled-in" disciples who provide shelter, food, and supplies for traveling missionaries. In order for the first type of disciple to survive and succeed, the second type of disciple must possess and provide.

There are two callings: one to leave behind family and possessions to further the cause in full-time ministry, and the other to serve Christ's cause in a home and community and to earn an income to support those whose calling means they can no longer generate sufficient income on their own. To determine which calling of God is ours, we should ask him for wisdom and guidance (James 1:5), realizing that he intends for us to know what his will is for us (Ephesians 5:17). We should seek wise counsel, knowing that the most important aspect of our lives is our closeness to our Master, not the specific places we go.

Both callings serve exactly the same purpose: glorifying God and furthering his Kingdom. Just because they have different lifestyles, one kind of disciple is neither more nor less spiritual than the other. (We should be careful not to discourage one another from *either* of these callings.)

Nowhere in Scripture, however, do we see a *third* kind of disciple who hoards and uses money and possessions as he pleases instead of for God's glory and Kingdom purposes.

What is expected of both goers and stayers?

Those who choose to follow Jesus aren't choosing an easy path: "If anyone would come after me, he must deny himself and take up his cross and follow me. For whoever wants to save his life will lose it, but whoever loses his life for me and for the gospel will save it. What good is it for a man to gain the whole world, yet forfeit his soul? Or what can a man give in exchange for his soul?" (Mark 8:34-37, NIV).

The number of economic terms Jesus uses here is striking: *save, lose, gain, forfeit, give,* and *exchange.* All disciples of Christ receive a radical call to view and handle our money and possessions with an eternal perspective.

We shouldn't be preoccupied with God's plan for others. When Peter asks Jesus about his plans for John, Jesus tells him, "If I want [John] to remain alive until I return, what is that to you? As for you, follow me" (John 21:22).

Nor should we make unhealthy comparisons. Paul

made this clear: "Pay careful attention to your own work, for then you will get the satisfaction of a job well done, and you won't need to compare yourself to anyone else. For we are each responsible for our own conduct" (Galatians 6:4-5).

In God's Kingdom, there's no room for comparing and judging others. We should recognize that God leads his children into differing spheres of Kingdom influence.

How much can we safely keep?

There are some things that no Christian should do—such as hoard money, live in opulence, or fail to give generously. But there are other things that some Christians can freely do that others may sense God's leading not to do, such as own land, a home, a car, or a business; go on certain vacations; or set aside significant retirement funds.

How much money and how many possessions can we safely keep? Enough to care for our basic needs and some wants, but not so much that large amounts of money are kept from higher Kingdom causes. Not so much that we become proud and independent of the Lord. Not so much that it distracts us from our purpose or leaves us with the illusion that we are owners rather than managers of what God owns.

Those who *happen* to be rich—simply as a result of circumstances, hard work, or wisdom—have done nothing wrong. They need not feel guilty—*unless* they withhold their riches (which are really God's) from Kingdom causes, including helping the needy, or their lifestyles are self-centered and excessive.

John Piper says in *Desiring God*, "The issue is not how much a person makes. Big industry and big salaries are a fact of our times, and they are not necessarily evil. The evil is in being deceived into thinking a $100,000 salary must be accompanied by a $100,000 lifestyle. God has made us to be conduits of his grace. The danger is in thinking the conduit should be lined with gold. It shouldn't. Copper will do."

What's the difference between a simple lifestyle and a strategic one?

Scripture says we're at war—it's a spiritual battle against unseen but very real enemies. "We are not fighting against flesh-and-blood enemies, but against evil rulers and authorities of the unseen world, against mighty powers in this dark world, and against evil spirits in the heavenly places" (Ephesians 6:12).

With this in mind, we should adopt lifestyles and make sacrifices commensurate to this crisis, so we may win the war.

Ralph Winter, founder of the U.S. Center for World Mission, used the term "wartime lifestyle." We might also call it a "strategic" lifestyle. I find that description more helpful and precise than "simple" lifestyle. If I'm devoted to "simple living," I might reject a computer because it's modern and nonessential. But if I live a wartime or strategic lifestyle, the computer may serve as a tool for Kingdom purposes. In my case, I use it daily to serve God in my writing. A microwave oven isn't essential. But it's handy and labor saving and can free up time to engage in Kingdom causes. Simple living may be self-centered. Strategic living is Kingdom centered.

Is it all right to own certain possessions for personal enjoyment?

A wartime mentality can be taken to such an extreme that we feel it's unfaithful to enjoy any possessions, pleasures, or special activities. I'm thankful that in the midst of his command that the rich be generous, Paul tells them to put their hope in God, "who richly gives us all we need for our enjoyment" (1 Timothy 6:17). Even in wartime, soldiers take leave when possible.

Our battle lasts a lifetime, so I'm grateful to have recreational items, including a bicycle and a tennis racket. Our family spends money on vacations that aren't "necessary" but serve to renew us. My wife and I sometimes go out to dinner, enriching our relationship. These things aren't essential, yet they contribute to physical health and mental and emotional refreshment. By God's grace, we've found that we can give away most of our income yet still have breathing room for legitimate recreational spending.

With a wartime mentality, we will not look at our income as God's call to spend more but rather as his provision to invest more in the cause. Why not set a financial "finish line," determining to live on a certain amount of money each year, an amount that allows some room for discretionary or recreational spending and reasonable saving? Then why not give all income beyond that to God's Kingdom purposes?

Nanci and I have sought, for the most part, to live that way the past twenty years. I know others who have made similar choices, while yet others have made far greater sacrifices. What may strike us as radical, when compared to those around us, even in our Christian culture, seems not to be radical at all when compared to the teaching of Scripture.

CHAPTER 16

Debt:
Finding Freedom
and Wisdom

Why is the topic of debt so important?
For many people, debt has become not the exception
but the rule.

The average American family devotes one-fourth of
its spendable income to outstanding debts. Since 1945,
consumer debt in the United States has multiplied
thirty-one times. The IRS calculates that the average
filer spends ten times more paying interest on debts
than he gives to charitable causes.

If all evangelical Christians were out of debt, hundreds of millions of dollars would be freed up for God's
Kingdom. Our families would be stronger, because
financial pressure caused by indebtedness is a major
factor in most divorces.

Home mortgages, auto loans, and credit cards all
seem normal to us, but in fact debt is an aberration
that evokes severe warnings from God's Word. We must

take a closer look at debt to understand the serious problem it poses.

One hundred years ago, debt was regarded as an earned privilege for the few—entrepreneurial business-people or farmers who faced hardship such as their crops being devastated by a tornado. Now it's seen as an inalienable right for all. Borrowing has become an integral part of our lives. Why do banks and credit companies repeatedly beg me to borrow from them, listing dozens of ways I could use the money? The answer is simple—they want me to borrow because they will profit greatly from my debt. In some cases I also may benefit, but in most cases, unless I have chosen very carefully, I will experience more harm than benefit.

Why does a credit card statement show a payment due of only $35 on a $500 balance? Because the less borrowers pay now, the more they have to pay later. If most people paid the full amount each month, lenders would go out of business.

The question for the Christian is this: How can we be fully free to serve God when we're serving human creditors?

Our debt-centered economy is like those electronic bug zappers. They emit a light attractive to insects that blissfully fly right into the trap.

"That's a cool-looking TV. And what a great sale! I don't have any cash. No problem. . . . Here's my MasterCard."

Zap!

Why should debt usually be avoided?

The Bible does not absolutely forbid debt, but it issues strong cautions concerning it. Debt is servitude: "Just as the rich rule the poor, so the borrower is servant to the lender" (Proverbs 22:7). But we're told, "You were bought with a price; do not become slaves of human masters" (1 Corinthians 7:23, NRSV). God says borrowers put themselves in servitude to lenders; then he tells us we should be slaves only to him, not men. Isn't that a powerful warning against going into debt?

The Mosaic law reflects a strong connection between debtors and slaves. So horrible was this situation—and so detrimental in the long term—that God commanded a Year of Jubilee every fifty years when debts would be canceled. More often than not, people were sold into slavery because they were unable to pay back debts. God had special provision for that, too—commanding freedom for slaves after six years: "This is how it must be done. Everyone must cancel the loans they have made to their fellow Israelites. They must not demand payment from their neighbors or relatives, for the LORD's time of release has arrived. . . . If a fellow Hebrew sells himself or herself to be your servant and serves you for six years, in the seventh year you must set that servant free" (Deuteronomy 15:2, 12).

In a time of famine in Israel, substantial debt was regarded as an act of great despair. People cried, "'We have mortgaged our fields, vineyards, and homes to get food during the famine.' And others said, 'We have had to borrow money on our fields and vineyards to pay our taxes. We belong to the same family as those who are wealthy, and our children are just like theirs. Yet we must sell our children into slavery just to get enough money to live. We have already sold some of our daughters, and we are helpless to do anything about it, for our fields and vineyards are already mortgaged to others'" (Nehemiah 5:3-5).

The assumption of the passage is that such things as mortgaging land and homes would *never* be done under normal circumstances.

God warned the people of Israel that disobedience would bring upon them the curse of being borrowers rather than lenders, subjecting them to the mastery of others: "They will lend money to you, but you will not lend to them. They will be the head, and you will be the tail!" (Deuteronomy 28:44). He also warned them not to take legal responsibility for others' debts: "Don't agree to guarantee another person's debt or put up security for someone else. If you can't pay it, even your bed will be snatched from under you" (Proverbs 22:26-27).

What else does the Bible say about debt?

The book of Proverbs warns those in debt to get out of debt's bondage as soon as possible.

The NASB translates Romans 13:8, "Owe nothing to anyone." This would appear to prohibit debt. The NIV reads, "Let no debt remain outstanding." This seems to allow debt but only if it is paid off as soon as possible.

Hudson Taylor and Charles Spurgeon believed that Romans 13:8 prohibits debt altogether. However, if going into debt is always sin, why does Scripture give guidelines about lending and even encourage lending under certain circumstances? If debt is always sin, then lending is aiding and abetting sin; surely God would never encourage it.

Unless there's an overwhelming need or a compelling rationale to borrow, it's unwise for God's children to put themselves under the curse of indebtedness. At the very least, Romans 13:8 proves we shouldn't *normally* borrow and we should always pay off debt as soon as possible.

- "The wicked borrow and never repay, but the godly are generous givers" (Psalm 37:21).
- "My husband who served you is dead, and you know how he feared the LORD. But now a creditor has come, threatening to take my two sons as slaves" (2 Kings 4:1).
- "When you are on the way to court with your adversary, settle your differences quickly. Otherwise, your accuser may hand you over to the judge, who will hand you over to an officer, and you will be thrown into prison. And if that happens, you surely won't be free again until you have paid the last penny" (Matthew 5:25-26).

If we take God's Word seriously, we should avoid debt when possible. In those rare cases where we go into debt, we should make every effort to get out as soon as we can.

We should never undertake debt without prayerful consideration and wise counsel. Our questions should be, *Why* go into debt? Is the risk called for? Will the benefits of becoming servants to the lender *really* outweigh the costs?

What should we ask ourselves before going into debt?

Before we incur debt, we should ask ourselves some basic spiritual questions: Is the fact that I don't have enough resources to pay cash for something God's way of telling me it isn't his will for me to buy it? Or is it possible that this thing may have been God's will but poor choices put me in a position where I can't afford to buy it? Wouldn't I do better to learn God's lesson by foregoing it until—by his provision and my diligence—I save enough money to buy it?

What I would call the "debt mentality" is a distorted perspective that involves invalid assumptions:

- We need more than God has given us.
- God doesn't know best what our needs are.
- God has failed to provide for our needs, forcing us to take matters into our own hands.
- If God doesn't come through the way we think he should, we can find another way.
- Just because today's income is sufficient to make

our debt payments, tomorrow's will be too (i.e., our circumstances won't change).

Those with convictions against borrowing will normally find ways to avoid it. Those without a firm conviction against going into debt will inevitably find the "need" to borrow.

The best credit risks are those who won't borrow in the first place. The more you're inclined to go into debt, the more probable it is that you shouldn't.

Ask yourself, "Is the money I'll be obligated to repay worth the value I'll receive by getting the money or possessions now? When it comes time for me to repay my debt, what new needs will I have that my debt will keep me from meeting? Or what new wants will I have that will tempt me to go further into debt?"

Consider these statements of God's Word:

- "True godliness with contentment is itself great wealth. After all, we brought nothing with us when we came into the world, and we can't take anything with us when we leave it. So if we have enough food and clothing, let us be content" (1 Timothy 6:6-8).
- "Those who love money will never have enough. How meaningless to think that wealth brings true happiness!" (Ecclesiastes 5:10).
- "My child, don't lose sight of common sense and discernment. Hang on to them, for they will refresh your soul. They are like jewels on

a necklace. They keep you safe on your way, and your feet will not stumble. You can go to bed without fear; you will lie down and sleep soundly. You need not be afraid of sudden disaster or the destruction that comes upon the wicked, for the LORD is your security. He will keep your foot from being caught in a trap" (Proverbs 3:21-26).

- "Don't copy the behavior and customs of this world, but let God transform you into a new person by changing the way you think. Then you will learn to know God's will for you, which is good and pleasing and perfect" (Romans 12:2).

It's one thing to trust God to provide for our present needs. It's another to presume upon him by dictating the terms of his future provision. Do we dare try to maneuver God into a position by which we significantly increase our future needs through debt, then claim he's promised to meet our needs?

In such cases, debt is not only unwise but evil. To expect God to meet needs we manufacture through indebtedness is an attempt to manipulate the Almighty. Assuming the role of master, we demote God to the obedient genie who exists to grant our wishes, underwrite our causes, and fulfill our agendas.

If debt has become your master, I highly recommend finding wise advisors. Consider the helpful resources available from people such as Dave Ramsey, Ron Blue, Matt Bell, Larry Burkett, and Howard Dayton.

What do wise money managers understand about spending and debt?

1. *Nothing is a good deal unless you can afford it.*
   Paying $220,000 for a house worth $270,000
   sounds like a great deal. But countless people
   step into financial bondage because they
   spend money they don't have in order to
   underwrite a "once in a lifetime opportunity."
   God is not behind every good deal! Self-control
   means turning down most good deals on
   things we want because God may have other
   and better plans for his money.

2. *You don't save money by spending money.*
   Saving money is setting it aside for a future
   purpose—it remains accessible to you.
   Spending money is making it disappear—so
   it's no longer at our disposal. If you buy
   an $80 sweater on sale for $30, how much
   do you save? Nothing. You spent $30. If
   you think buying things on sale is "saving"
   money, keep it up and you'll go broke!

3. *Just because you can afford something doesn't*
   mean God wants you to buy it. Remember,
   God usually grants us excess not to find new
   ways to spend it but in order to give to others
   in need (2 Corinthians 8:14).

4. *Every purchase should be examined in light*
   of its alternative uses or ministry potential.

Before we spend $20, $100, or $1,000 on something, we should weigh the value of our purchases against what the same money could have done if used another way.

5. *We should understand and resist the manipulative nature of advertising.* Responsible spending says yes to real needs and no to most "created" needs. Advertising thrives on instilling discontent. People have master's degrees in persuading us to buy things we don't need.

6. *Little expenses add up to big problems.* Like water from a leaky faucet, money trickles through our hands. The little drips don't seem like much, but they add up to gallons. One dollar here and ten dollars over there; a hamburger here, a mocha there; video rentals, a round of golf, extra tools, new clothes. If a swimming pool is full of leaks, you can pump in more water (bring in more income), but it will never be enough until you find the leaks and fix them.

Have you learned how to set a budget and live on it?

Imagine you've entrusted a large sum to a money manager, telling him to take out only what he needs to live on and then invest the bulk of it on your behalf. A few months later, you call him to see how your investments are doing. He says, "There are no investments. None of your money is left." Shocked, you ask, "Where did it all go?" Sheepishly, your money manager responds, "Well, I can think of some expenses here and there, but . . . one thing led to another and before I knew it, it was all gone!"

What would you think? How would you feel? How does God feel when at the end of the month nothing's left from the money he entrusted to us, and we don't even know where it went? If some of us ran a corporation and handled its money like we do God's, we'd go to prison!

"Be sure you know the condition of your flocks, give careful attention to your herds; for riches do not endure forever" (Proverbs 27:23-24, NIV). God is saying to all of us, know what your assets are and know where they go.

We must get a grip on our management of God's assets. If we don't have well-thought-out plans for what to do with God's money, rest assured: Others do.

Two practical steps can greatly help us get a grip on our spending: recording expenditures and making a budget. They will foster a healthy dialogue about what we do with our money and help us develop careful spending habits.

Many people are kept from unwise decisions simply by knowing they have to record them for themselves, their spouse, or a financial advisor. God tells us he will hold us accountable for our money management—so we should hold ourselves accountable and enlist others to help us do the same. This will improve our mental and marital health, since financial disorder is one of the leading causes of personal and familial stress and often results in divorce.

Larry Burkett's *Family Budget Workbook* has been around many years, and many people have found it helpful.

Have you learned to wait upon the Lord?

How often do we take matters into our own hands and spend impulsively without asking God to furnish the item for us? How often do we buy something a week or a month before God would have provided it for free or at minimal cost, if only we'd asked him and waited on him? If he doesn't provide it, fine—he knows best. Why don't we pray and give him a chance?

Why not discipline yourself not to buy unless you've wanted something over a period of time? Waiting eliminates most impulsive buying. I've found that many things which attract me today hold no interest three months later. Look at garage sales, and you get the picture. Setting a waiting period gives God the opportunity to provide what we want, to provide something different or better, or to show us that we don't need it and should use the money differently.

People say, "I'll just fill out the loan application. If it goes through, I'll take that as a sign God wants me to borrow the money." But just because a lender is willing to give us a loan doesn't mean God approves of our decision to borrow, as a clerk's willingness to sell us a lottery ticket doesn't indicate that God approves of our gambling.

Matthew 6:33 suggests God will provide for our basic material needs if we seek first his Kingdom. But nowhere does he promise to repay for all the debts we acquire through our own greed, impatience, or presumption. In this age where we seem unwilling to wait for anything, God may desire us to discipline ourselves and stay out of debt mainly to learn to "wait on the Lord" (Psalm 27:14, NKJV; Isaiah 30:18). When we wait for him instead of rushing ahead of him, we'll be amazed at what he provides and what we learn in the process.

CHAPTER 17

Questions and Answers about Debt

JESUS TOLD US what is more important than anything else: "You shall love the Lord your God with all your heart and with all your soul and with all your mind. This is the great and first commandment. And a second is like it: You shall love your neighbor as yourself" (Matthew 22:37–39, ESV).

Accordingly, God says there is one debt to which all our money and possessions must be unreservedly committed, yet which we can never retire: "Owe nothing to anyone—except for your obligation to love one another. If you love your neighbor, you will fulfill the requirements of God's law" (Romans 13:8).

Our indebtedness to God is to be treated as indebtedness to others so that we keep both God and others in mind as we manage his money. In order to best fulfill that spiritual debt, we must free ourselves from the burdens that come with financial debt.

What about borrowing to buy a house?

Many financial counselors put home mortgages in a different category from other debts. One reason is that the loan is secured by the house's equity. If financial crises arise and the payments can't be made, the home can be sold and the equity—which is the current sale value of the house minus the amount still owed on the mortgage—can be regained.

A case can certainly be made for borrowing to buy a reasonably priced house instead of renting. Nanci and I did this many years ago, accelerating our payments and paying off the thirty-year contract in fifteen years. We've never regretted borrowing the money or paying off the loan early, which greatly reduced the cost and positioned us well when one month after our final house payment we experienced the loss of my job and a significant long-term decrease in monthly income.

Unfortunately, many aspiring homeowners end up buying a house that's out of their price range. We all need shelter, but do we need a particular house in a certain neighborhood? We all need food, but do we need to eat out so often? We need clothes, but do we need designer labels? Look at the words of Jesus and Paul: "Guard against every kind of greed. Life is not measured by how much you own" (Luke 12:15); "I have learned how to be content with whatever I have. . . . I have learned the secret of living in every situation, whether it is with a full stomach or empty, with plenty or little" (Philippians 4:11-12).

Houses are often considered a primary exception to the "stay out of debt" rule since most purchases are high-depreciation items, including cars, clothes, and furniture. As soon as we buy such things, we typically cannot turn around and sell them without a significant loss. For instance, the moment you sign to buy a new car, you lose thousands of dollars in resale value that you cannot recoup. The steeper the depreciation, the greater the risk in a purchase and the greater our presumption that we can absorb the loss it entails.

For years, many people believed that houses *always* appreciate, that money put into a house was like money put into the bank—yet in recent years, as many have experienced firsthand, house values have plunged. God and his principles are certain. The economy is not. Who can know for sure which assets will appreciate?

A reasonably priced house with affordable payments *may* be a wise investment. But not always. We need to get the stars out of our eyes and think realistically before taking on the extensive debt involved in home ownership.

The monthly payment for a home mortgage, including taxes and insurance, shouldn't be much more than buyers are willing to pay for rent. Most of the monthly mortgage payment goes for interest, but there are tax deductions that will reduce the net cost. Money paid for rent isn't tax deductible and doesn't build equity; on the other hand, homeowners spend far more on fixtures, decorations, upkeep, and improvements.

One common formula for figuring out what's

affordable is a purchase price that's two-and-a-half times (or less) the family's gross annual income. But remember, there's no guarantee that you will have your job next year or that you will make as much money. Bottom line, borrowing for a home is *sometimes* wise and sometimes not.

If debt seems the best or a necessary choice, go slowly and prayerfully. Get objective financial counsel from good stewards (Proverbs 15:22). Some real estate agents give helpful counsel, but many won't advise you objectively since they are rewarded if you overspend. Husbands and wives should be sure they're in total agreement, or their marriage will pay the price.

Should we have and use credit cards?

As of 2010, the average American credit card holder owed over $8,000 to credit card companies. And while those with extreme debt pull that average up, it's equally true that those who pay off their cards in full every month pull it down. The average college student owes about $20,000 in student loans by graduation, some three times that much, plus another $3,000 in credit card debt on nonessentials.

Credit cards facilitate impulse buying, typically for unnecessary and self-indulgent purchases. When using credit, consumers buy more, buy what they don't need, and pay more for it.

Like being handed the controls of a deadly weapon with a hair trigger, many people are propelled by their credit cards into irresponsible debt that entails exorbitant interest, often 15 to 20 percent annually. (Even when it's under 10 percent, it adds up quickly.) The person with a $2,000 balance (at 19.5 percent interest) is told he can pay just $75. But he doesn't realize that the first $32.50 of that $75 is interest! He goes right on charging "sale" items and digging an ever deeper hole.

If you carry a $7,000 balance on an 18 percent credit card and pay the 2 percent minimum payment each month, you'll end up paying more than $20,000 for that $7,000. All those things you bought at half price? They may cost you three times what you think they did.

Some people use credit cards for the convenience, paying off the full amount owed on every statement so they don't ever pay interest costs. We do this ourselves, and in twenty-five years we have never paid any interest. This approach has advantages, but it also has drawbacks. Citibank calculates that a consumer using a credit card will buy 26 percent more than he would if he were carrying cash, even if he pays it all off without interest charges.

Here are some simple rules:

- Never use your credit cards for anything except budgeted purchases.
- Pay your balance in full *every* month.
- The first month you have a credit card bill you cannot pay in full, perform plastic surgery—cut the card in half and don't get another one.

Even if you pay the full amount when due and avoid interest charges, if it's psychologically easier for you to lay down a credit card than to part with cash, you shouldn't own a credit card. If you carry a credit card and say, "I won't use it except for emergencies when I would have used cash anyway," you may minimize the drawbacks. But keep an eye on your spending. The ancient book of Proverbs applies directly to our use of credit cards: "A prudent person foresees danger and takes precautions. The simpleton goes blindly on and suffers the consequences" (Proverbs 22:3).

When it comes to credit cards, be wise, not foolish.

Should we pay off all debts before giving money to God?

Responsibility to God is not negated by our choices to become indebted to men. When we rob God to pay men, we rob ourselves of God's blessing. No wonder we don't have enough when we are holding on to what God called on us to give to him. It's a vicious cycle, and it takes obedient faith to break out of it.

Even if I've come into debt legitimately, isn't my first debt to God since he says that the firstfruits belong to him and not to me?

For Christians today, firstfruits are the first portion of what we've earned: "On the first day of each week, you should each put aside a portion of the money you have earned. Don't wait . . ." (1 Corinthians 16:2).

If we're faithful in our giving to God, only then can

we look to him for help in finding the resources to pay others. Jesus says in Luke 6:38 that with the measure we give to God it will be given back to us. Now, this doesn't mean generous givers never experience business losses. But it does mean that God will sustain faithful givers even in the midst of financial difficulty. And the more serious our financial problems, the more critical it is that we do what God ensures will result in his provision—give!

God will not eliminate the consequences of our unwise decisions. If by giving to God we can no longer afford to make payments on a loan, then we need to liquidate our assets, take losses where we must, and pay off that debt. But we should never rob God—not for any reason, and certainly not to compensate for past or present self-indulgence.

How can we get out of debt?

Scripture declares that whether we borrow for good reasons or bad, it's our responsibility to pay it back as soon as possible. To not repay a debt is to join ranks with the wicked: "The wicked borrow and never repay, but the godly are generous givers" (Psalm 37:21). Bankruptcy, though lawful, is normally not a moral option. I believe God is honored when people of integrity come out of bankruptcy proceedings with the legal right not to pay back a dime, but as a matter of conscience, dedicate themselves to full repayment as soon as they can.

If you are in debt, two questions are relevant: How

did you get into debt, and how can you get out? If you've gotten into debt unwisely, you should do more than get out of debt; you should also recognize that you've made wrong choices and commit yourself not to repeat them. Debt isn't the main problem; it's a symptom of a more basic problem—greed, impulsiveness, and lack of discipline—sins we must confess to God.

Here are eight steps I recommend to get out of debt:

1. *Repent.* Acknowledge that you've taken your cues from the world, not God. Change your mind and your actions regarding money, things, needs, wants, giving, saving, spending, and debt.

2. *Immediately give God the firstfruits.* When we give to God the first and best of our income, we say in effect to him, "I recognize your ownership and trust you to bless my obedience." It's self-contradictory to seek God's blessing on your finances while putting yourself under his curse by withholding the tithe (and even the freewill offerings) he directs you to give.

3. *Incur no new debts.* Operate on this principle: "If I can't afford it now, it isn't God's will now."

4. *Systematically eliminate existing debts.* Prepare a realistic budget. Make a specific plan to get out of debt. Seek wise financial counsel. Liquidate unnecessary assets. It won't

happen overnight, but with a good plan and determination you can and will get out of debt.

5. *Perform plastic surgery on your credit cards.* If the card makes spending easier or you can't pay the balance in full each month, cut it up.

6. *Stop rationalizing your debt habit.* Houses and cars are the strongest temptations for some, whereas furniture, clothing, or electronic equipment tempts others. Recognize your weakness, and don't let it master you. When it comes to houses, remember this: The Carpenter of Nazareth is making the perfect home for you in Heaven (John 14:2-3). It's not here and now; it's then and there! Consider that God may want you to use his money here and now to send building materials ahead (Matthew 6:19-21).

7. *List your debts and, if necessary, contact your creditors.* Establish a schedule that's workable within your budget to repay your creditors. By comparing the different interest rates on your debts, prioritize your debt reduction, then pay off most quickly those with the highest interest. If your debt is beyond your ability to pay at prescribed levels, explain your plan of repayment to your creditors. Normally they will welcome your plan, because they're often faced with bankruptcies in which they receive little or nothing. In

some areas you can contact the Consumer Credit Counseling Service, which offers debt counseling at no cost. (But if they advise you to stop giving to God's Kingdom until you're out of debt, remember, robbing God isn't a solution; it's a major part of the problem.)

8. If you've done everything else and there still isn't enough money, *consider new ways to increase your income.* (I've been assuming you are doing all you can to work for a living and earn a wage; if you aren't, obviously, that's where you should start.) Liquidate unnecessary assets, and use the funds to reduce debt. If you are already working full-time, more work isn't a long-term solution. Still, a second job or household business may be a temporary necessity to reverse the consequences of past decisions.

Be patient. It may have taken you years, even decades, to accumulate debt. It won't disappear overnight. Remember, seek wise counsel. We get into financial trouble by acting on our own. We should expect to get out of it by doing the same.

By following these guidelines, you'll be well on your way out of bondage. You'll also start to experience the freedom to respond generously to needs and eternal investment opportunities. Your return on those investments will be the joy of giving, as well as God's grace and blessing that come with it.

CHAPTER 18

Preparing for the Future: Savings Accounts and Retirement Funds

THE PURPOSE OF saving is to set money aside for the future. By foregoing expenditures now, we preserve resources for later.

The wise anticipate future needs while the foolish consume their resources without forethought. Proverbs 21:20 says, "Fools spend whatever they get."

Why is the topic of saving important?

Nurserymen, carpenters, and others may produce seasonal incomes and must discipline themselves to save for the lean months. But most of us receive a regular paycheck. It seems wise to set aside funds to allow for both anticipated and unanticipated expenses—yet most people don't.

If the reason for this lack of savings were faith in God and a conviction that we shouldn't hang on to resources but give them to meet others' needs, then we'd be in good company with the poor widow of Mark 12 and the Macedonian Christians of 2 Corinthians 8. But the reason is usually self-indulgence, presumption, and lack of foresight and discipline.

"Take a lesson from the ants, you lazybones. Learn from their ways and become wise! Though they have no prince or governor or ruler to make them work, they labor hard all summer, gathering food for the winter" (Proverbs 6:6-8). Even ants know there will be no food in winter unless it's stored during the summer. Only a shortsighted person would fail to store up provisions (money, food, supplies) for upcoming times of predictable need.

By God's inspiration, Joseph devised a careful savings plan in anticipation of an upcoming famine in Egypt (Genesis 41:25-57). For seven years Egyptians stored 20 percent of the harvest. When the seven years of famine came, they drew on their stores of grain. Having anticipated future need and prepared for it, the nation was able to care for itself—and provide for others as well.

Lack of planning invites poverty. To feast now without regard to future famine is to manage our resources poorly and presume upon God or others to bail us out.

We must learn to weigh our expenditures not only in light of their immediate value but also their ultimate cost. Money needlessly spent is a double loss. Not only is it gone, but its *potential* for earnings disappears. Had we set it aside, it *could* have been multiplying on Earth through savings or in Heaven through giving.

It's wise to give first, save second, and spend last.

Otherwise, we will spend everything and have nothing to give or save, setting ourselves up to fall into debt when true needs arise. Saving is a discipline that develops authority over money.

After I give the firstfruits to the Lord, I can take money off the top of my paycheck to save for future purposes. I might save for a family vacation or a remodeling project. I'm not saving without purpose but for a specific cause.

Long-term savings can use years of plenty to prepare for years of decreased income. Projecting decreased income, I might set aside money to supplement it. Or I might systematically save for my children's college education, which could be ten years away.

Is saving ever wrong?

Some save in the wise way that Proverbs encourages. Some save out of greed, others because they're misers.

Still others save out of fear. By stockpiling money, they insulate themselves from God, no longer depending on his provision and protection.

Therefore we can't say, "Saving money is always biblical" or "Saving money is always unbiblical." It may be either, depending on the reasons and the alternatives.

Hoarding is saving taken to an extreme—accumulating great reserves for no purpose other than to ward off future disaster or to provide wealth for many years to come. The classic example of hoarding is the barn builder we met in chapter 1, who is also known as "the rich fool." God said of him, "A person is a fool to store up earthly wealth but not have a rich relationship with God" (Luke 12:18-21).

When we read about the rich fool, our first mistake is in distancing ourselves from him. Because we know so many people who are wealthier than we are, we imagine we're not rich. But we're wrong.

Enter your annual income into the wealth calculator at www.globalrichlist.com. If you made $50,000 last year, you're in the top one percent of the world's wealthy. If you made $25,000, you're in the top 10 percent. But even if you made only $1,500 last year, believe it or not, you would still have made *more money than 75 percent of all people on Earth.* (Don't let this mislead you if you're young and living off your parents' money. Your income may be small, but you have access to remarkable wealth.)

We must realize that when Scripture speaks of the rich, it is not talking about "them" but "us." If we are rich (and we *are*), we aren't necessarily living in sin. But we are certainly under great *temptation* to sin. And most rich people succumb to that temptation.

Our second mistake in reading about the rich fool is in assuming we're not fools. But read what the passage actually says—he was simply living out the American dream as reflected in television commercials, movies, and conversations. He was storing up wealth to rely on in the future while enjoying his favorite recreational pursuits.

Ask yourself these tough questions: "In the way that I live, in the financial choices I make, including my giving, am I more like the poor widow of Mark 12 whom Jesus commended, or the rich fool of Luke 12, whom Jesus condemned? What can I do to become more like one and less like the other?"

How can we approach saving with biblical balance?

Saving for possible short-term needs can be wise, whereas saving vast sums for decades ahead can be foolish. This may appear inconsistent, but I'm attempting to balance what Scripture says about both. We can't ignore all the verses in Proverbs that laud saving, yet neither can we ignore Christ's scathing appraisal of the rich fool. Personally, I find balancing the two very difficult—but that's the position Scripture puts us in. The solution is to affirm and honor both groups of Scripture, not ignore one.

A common goal of hoarders is to achieve "financial independence." But from whom do we wish to be independent? God? Our family? Christian brothers and sisters? I certainly favor independence from the government or parents, in the sense that I earn my own living. There's a kind of dependence that's terribly unhealthy. But isn't there a kind of independence that's equally unhealthy?

Proverbs declares, "Trust in your money and down you go!" (11:28). And the New Testament clearly teaches that we are to be *channels* of money and possessions, not storehouses. Whatever role saving has in our lives, it should always be secondary to giving. And it must never be a substitute for trusting God.

Read carefully what James says about the rich (and remember, that's us):

> Look here, you rich people: Weep and groan
> with anguish because of all the terrible troubles
> ahead of you. Your wealth is rotting away,
> and your fine clothes are moth-eaten rags.
> Your gold and silver have become worthless.
> The very wealth you were counting on will
> eat away your flesh like fire. This treasure
> you have accumulated will stand as evidence
> against you on the day of judgment. For listen!
> Hear the cries of the field workers whom you
> have cheated of their pay. The wages you held
> back cry out against you. The cries of those
> who harvest your fields have reached the ears
> of the LORD of Heaven's Armies. You have
> spent your years on earth in luxury, satisfying
> your every desire. You have fattened yourselves
> for the day of slaughter. (James 5:1-5)

James suggests it was rich people's hoarding and self-indulgence that assured their bleak future under God's coming judgment. Contrary to human logic, hoarding doesn't avoid future problems; it causes them!

When God provided manna from Heaven to meet the needs of his people, he told them they'd have just enough for each day.

"These are the LORD's instructions: Each household should gather as much as it needs. Pick up two quarts for each person in your tent." So the people of Israel did as they were told. Some gathered a lot, some only a little. But when they measured it out, everyone had just enough. Those who gathered a lot had nothing left over, and those who gathered only a little had enough. Each family had just what it needed. Then Moses told them, "Do not keep any of it until morning." But some of them didn't listen and kept some of it until morning. But by then it was full of maggots and had a terrible smell. Moses was very angry with them. (Exodus 16:16-20)

Notice that some of the Israelites kept manna until the next day, determined to save up in case God didn't come through. But God made the stored manna foul, filling it with maggots. If we successfully accumulate large reserves against the future rather than meet present world needs, God will be displeased.

God promises provision for his obedient, responsible, and wise children who seek first his Kingdom (Matthew 6:30-34).

When I save, I lay something aside for future need. But I hold it loosely, realizing it's all at God's disposal. If I sense God's leading, I will give it away to meet greater needs. When I hoard, I'm unwilling to part with what I've saved to meet others' needs because my possible future needs outweigh their actual present needs. Hence, I fail to love my neighbor as myself.

Is retirement biblical, and how much money is enough?

When a man retires at sixty-five, studies show his chances of having a fatal heart attack immediately double. Our minds and bodies weren't made to be shut down. Nowhere in Scripture do we see God calling healthy people to stop working. So before we think about saving for retirement, we should reexamine our thinking about retirement itself. How much of what we think and assume is based on our culture, and how much is really based on God's Word and the leading of his Holy Spirit?

Of course, it's perfectly legitimate to work without pay. You might donate labor to ministries and volunteer. But as long as God has us in this world, he has work for us to do. The hours may be shorter, the work different, the pay lower or nonexistent. But he doesn't want us to take still-productive minds and bodies and permanently lay them on a beach, lose them on a golf course, or lock them in a dark living room watching game shows.

Is saving large amounts of money for retirement as essential as we're constantly told? Paul commended the Macedonian believers, not for clinging to the little they had, but for giving beyond their means (2 Corinthians 8:3-5).

The Macedonian Christians had virtually no

material things, yet they gave beyond their means to the point of leaving themselves impoverished. If they didn't need to think of tomorrow, why do we—with all our material wealth—need to be so concerned about storing up earthly treasures for thirty years from now?

I'm not saying we can't use or shouldn't have retirement plans—but as God's children, we don't *need* them. Our brothers and sisters in other ages didn't have them, and neither do most non-American Christians today. Yet they've found God absolutely sufficient to meet their needs. Usually the wealthy are most consumed by retirement planning simply because they have the resources to think in those terms.

Nanci's and my retirement savings are very small by American standards but very large by global standards. How much is too much? I can't answer that question for you. I have a hard enough time trying to figure it out for myself. But I do know that each of us should ask God because the money we are dealing with belongs to him, not us. We should shut out the distracting noises of the world, tune our ears to God's Word, and quietly listen for his answer.

Is anything "hands off" to God?

My conversations with many Christians over the years prompt me to say something else: If you're holding on to money today with the thought that by keeping it you'll have more to give later, you're kidding yourself. The economy may fail, or you may become dependent on the money you've held on to and your heart will stay on Earth with your money instead of following it to Heaven. *Nongivers remain nongivers until the moment they give.* Money earmarked for future giving cannot fulfill its purpose as long as we hold on to it. Actions, not intentions, define givers.

Our accumulated financial reserves and valuable possessions should all be considered fair game for divine distribution. We should be especially quick to evaluate luxury items. What could be accomplished if jewelry that sits in a box were sold and the money given to the needy, world evangelism, church planting, and Bible translation? Antiques, art, coins, and other collections may be of great (but only temporary) financial worth. They could be used for strategic purpose in the Kingdom of God—but not when they're sitting in a safe, behind a locked display, or hanging on a wall.

Is God calling us to liquidate some of these items and invest them in his Kingdom? Are we willing to seek his will in diligent prayer and biblical meditation? If anything we have is off limits to God, if it's not subject to prayerful dialogue, then let's be honest about it—we aren't stewards; we're embezzlers. We aren't *serving* God; we're *playing* God.

If we consider "our" retirement funds off limits to God, we're pretending to be owners rather than God's money managers. When we ask God's direction for our lives, we need to lay everything on the table. Whatever posture I take with financial planning must leave room—a great deal of room—for God.

At the conclusion of the movie *Schindler's List*, there's a heart-wrenching scene in which Oskar Schindler—who saved many Jews from the Nazis—looks at his car and his gold pin and regrets that he didn't give up more of his money and possessions to save more lives. Schindler had used his opportunity far better than most. But in the end, he longed for a chance to go back and choose human lives over material possessions.

Just as unbelievers have no second chance to relive their lives, this time choosing Christ, Christians get no second chance to live life over, the second time doing more to help the needy and invest in God's Kingdom. We have one brief opportunity—a lifetime on Earth—to use our resources to make a difference.

John Wesley said, "I judge all things only by the price they shall gain in eternity." Missionary C. T. Studd said, "Only one life, 'twill soon be past; only what's done for Christ will last."

Five minutes after we die, we'll know exactly how we should have lived. But God has given us his Word so we don't have to wait to die to find out. And he's given us his Spirit to empower us to live that way now.

In this light, ask yourself, "What will I one day wish I would have given away while I still had the chance?" When you come up with an answer, why not give it away *now*? Why not spend the rest of your life closing the gap between what you'll *wish* you'd given and what you really *are* giving?

CHAPTER 19

Looking for Returns: Gambling and Investing

THERE'S A DIFFERENCE between gambling and taking *reasonable* risks, including some investments. In gambling, wealth isn't earned or distributed on the basis of work, service, or personal need, but by chance. The goal is not to be productive but to "get lucky." But in God's plan, it's hard and wise work, not chance, that brings financial profit. The book of Proverbs says, "Lazy people want much but get little, but those who work hard will prosper. . . . Work brings profit, but mere talk leads to poverty!" (Proverbs 13:4; 14:23).

Is gambling okay?

A bumper sticker reads, "The lottery is a tax on people who are bad at math." You have a smaller chance of winning a multimillion-dollar lottery than of being struck by lightning.

One of the great ironies of gambling is that the vast majority of people lose money, while the few who win discover money doesn't make them happy—and often it actually ruins their lives! One study reported that "six months after winning the lottery, you are likely to be no happier than if you had been paralyzed in a car crash."

God says clearly, "You must not have any other god but me" (Exodus 20:3). To trust in gambling is to worship an idol. Only Jesus should be our Master. God tells us to work for a living, not play the odds and seek shortcuts to wealth (Proverbs 28:19-20). God is sufficient to supply all our needs (Philippians 4:19).

Ads for the Illinois lottery, posted on billboards in Chicago's poorest neighborhoods, read, "This could be your ticket out." It's unethical—and an offense to God—to tempt the poor to squander what little money they have. Dispensing false hope merely exploits them.

Card games that involve gambling have become very popular in the culture at large. Many Christians now view gambling as innocent fun. For some it probably is, but for others it is a doorway leading to addiction, obsession, and self-destruction. Gambling is a destroyer of marriages and families. How many people who start gambling as harmless fun with friends do not stop there but end up in ruin? And how many Christians will one day regret having introduced friends to gambling at their innocent weekly poker game?

God will reward his children for working hard at any honest job, earning money, using it wisely, and sharing it generously. Can you picture Jesus rewarding you for the time and money you spent gambling? What will be your reward for introducing others to it, including those who become addicted? "Our goal is to please him. For we must all stand before Christ to be judged. We will each receive whatever we deserve for the good or evil we have done in this earthly body" (2 Corinthians 5:9-10).

How does investing differ from gambling?

Although gambling often violates biblical principles, there are other actions in life that involve risk but are still legitimate. Scripture doesn't directly teach that we should invest, but it does provide illustrations of investing, including real estate ventures. The honored woman of Proverbs 31 "goes to inspect a field and buys it; with her earnings she plants a vineyard" (verse 16). Jesus speaks illustratively of investing in such a way as to gain financial returns (Matthew 25:14-29; Luke 19:12-26). His injunctions to invest in eternity by laying up treasures in Heaven rather than on Earth put our earthly investments in perspective but do not preclude them.

Can we be wiser about where we invest God's money?

Investing doesn't simply bring profits to the investor. It also profits the business in which we invest. A Christian should avoid investing in any enterprise that makes its profit from immoral practices. Mutual funds, today's most common investment vehicles, distribute their investors' money in a wide range of companies.

Many Christians don't evaluate the source of their

mutual funds' income. This certainly isn't easy when there are so many companies with so many names. Most Christians would think it was wrong to invest in *Playboy* magazine. But the Houston-based Internet company Telescan specializes in data retrieval tools that it uses in partnership with *Playboy*'s Web sites.

Consider Paul's words to two separate churches about being careful regarding partnerships: "Don't team up with those who are unbelievers. How can righteousness be a partner with wickedness? How can light live with darkness? . . . Take no part in the worthless deeds of evil and darkness; instead, expose them" (2 Corinthians 6:14; Ephesians 5:11).

It will not be easy, but if we are God's money managers, we should take responsibility to investigate—and choose carefully—where we put God's money. Though I've withdrawn from one mutual fund because of companies it supported, I realize that other funds we're invested in may include immoral holdings. I don't have the time or expertise to do extensive research and have only acted on information I've received. Most of us need to rely on others for this. To find out more, I recommend *Kingdom Gains* by Dwight Short and *Good Returns* by George P. Schwartz.

Some of our retirement funds are invested in a company whose guiding principles state that it "avoids investing in companies that are involved in practices contrary to Judeo-Christian principles," in particular abortion and pornography. Some years, this particular fund has underperformed the Standard & Poor's

500, and in others it has outperformed it. We have stayed with it in the low-performing years because we believe in its commitment to never fund what dishonors Christ.

Have you received and heeded wise counsel before investing?

A Christian investment firm held a seminar at a nearby Christian college. They presented a surefire investment opportunity too good to pass up. A couple in our church, along with many others, invested their entire savings. Not long afterward, the Christian investor and his Christian company disappeared with everyone's Christian money. This is tragic yet common. I've heard the same story, with different names and places, over and over again.

As Christians we want to believe the best, and we can be gullible as well as greedy. When a Christian businessman tells you he has a surefire investment that will multiply your money five times while you sleep, you might ask yourself why he needs your money. Why haven't savvy investors and knowledgeable lending institutions lined up outside his door to put their money into it? Likely because it is high risk and, all things considered, a very poor investment.

We should seek a number of counselors, not just one, when we're making important decisions. "Plans go wrong for lack of advice; many advisers bring success" (Proverbs 15:22).

The point isn't just quantity of counsel, but quality—advisors must be not just persuasive but truly wise: "Better to hear the quiet words of a wise person than the shouts of a foolish king" (Ecclesiastes 9:17).

Because wisdom begins with fearing God (Proverbs 9:10), usually these counselors should be Christians who you *know* are walking with God and living by his principles (never assume this based simply on nice-sounding words). No matter how strong someone's profession of faith, the counsel of the ungodly should never sway us (Psalm 1:1). Having weighed the Scriptures and sought judicious counsel, we should seek God's wisdom. He promises to give it to those who ask (James 1:5).

Many people sincerely desire to make profitable investments now and give substantial amounts to God's work later. I have often been asked, "Rather than give now, shouldn't I hang on to the money, hoping my investments will do well and I'll have more to give to God's Kingdom in five or ten years?"

In some cases this appears to have been wise. But my observation over many years is that countless good intentions are never realized. That leads me to say this: If you postpone giving, aren't you postponing God's blessing? If your heart goes where you put your treasure, are you putting your treasure on Earth, not Heaven? Shouldn't you give now to be sure the money goes to God's Kingdom? Considering the market may plummet, your heart my change, or you may die, by holding onto this money now, are you willing to risk that it will never end up where God wanted you to put it?

CHAPTER 20

Inheritance or Heritage: What to Leave Behind and What to Send Ahead

IN OLD TESTAMENT TIMES, it was essential that parents pass land ownership to their children and grandchildren. Many people were too poor to buy land. With no inheritance, they would end up enslaved or unable to care for their parents and grandparents, who normally lived on the property with them. Hence they were told, "A good man leaves an inheritance for his children's children" (Proverbs 13:22, NIV).

What's different about inheritances in our culture?

Today in America and many other affluent countries, inheritances are usually windfalls coming to people who

- live separately from their parents;
- have regular sources of income generated by their own work, skills, saving, and investing; and

- have far more than they need. Even if they are managing the family business, a windfall isn't needed for them to continue.

When such people inherit a farm, house, or other real estate, what becomes of it? Typically, they sell it. The inheritance doesn't enhance their work; it simply increases their standard of living, sometimes dramatically.

I consider it important not to leave money to our daughters that would interfere with my sons-in-law's responsibility to provide for them. Fortunately, my sons-in-law are very responsible, and I trust them fully. But how dare any of us, whether family or friends or government, allow our financial subsidies to deny the character-building privilege and divine calling of a man to work hard to provide for his wife and children?

Many well-meaning parents have caused serious marital conflicts by leaving money to their grown children. Money that's "his" and "hers" divides the marriage and fosters an unhealthy independence.

People often testify of the character, discipline, self-control, and trust in God they developed when they were younger and had much less to live on. How ironic that these same people pass on large amounts of money to their children, robbing them of similar blessings and character development.

Multimillionaire Andrew Carnegie said, "The almighty dollar bequeathed to a child is an almighty curse. No man has the right to handicap his son with such a burden as great wealth. He must face this question squarely: Will my fortune be safe with my boy and will my boy be safe with my fortune?"

Cornelius Vanderbilt said, "Inherited wealth is as certain death to ambition as cocaine is to morality." Henry Ford stated, "Fortunes tend to self-destruction by destroying those who inherit them."

More important, God says, "An inheritance quickly gained at the beginning will not be blessed at the end" (Proverbs 20:21, NIV).

Certainly we should not transfer wealth to adult children unless we've successfully transferred wisdom to them. Without wisdom, wealth will not only be wasted, but it will damage our children by subsidizing addictions, laziness, and immorality.

For many years I've had the opportunity to speak to and interact with wealthy believers, and I've heard heartbreaking stories about the devastating effects of receiving a large inheritance. In *The Legacy of Inherited Wealth,* compiled by two wealthy heiresses, seventeen adult heirs recount the blessings and curses of their inherited wealth. Their stories suggest that the curses far outweigh the blessings. What repeatedly surfaces is frustration, anger, doubt, insecurity, and resentment— all tied to growing up wealthy or becoming wealthy through inheritance.

The larger the estate, the more its potential for harm to those who inherit it. Wise parents can leave enough to their children and grandchildren to be helpful without leaving them so much as to hurt them.

Of course, besides preventing harm to our children, there is great good we can do by leaving money to God-exalting ministries. Any family members who would pout about or fight over what belonged to their deceased parents or who respond negatively when we decide to leave most of our money to the cause of Christ instead of to them prove they're unqualified to inherit in the first place. Such children need prayer and guidance. What they certainly do *not* need is more money.

If parents decide to give most or all of their estate to God's Kingdom, they should explain their plans to their children. This will prevent false expectations and free their children from later resentment. It will also alleviate present guilt feelings stemming from what children might imagine they have to gain by their parents' death. Even though they know they shouldn't, grown children commonly find themselves thinking about and looking forward to all the money and possessions that will be theirs when their parents die. Some go into debt now because they expect to, so to speak, win the lottery through their parents' deaths. The sooner these attitudes are defused, the better.

I recommend either having a family conference or writing out in detail what your plan is, then asking each adult child to get back to you with his or her response.

Committed Christians, whose parents declare their intent to leave most of their estate to God's work, will be the first to say, "That's wonderful, Dad and Mom. Go for it! And thanks for being a great example to us."

A wealthy man told me that he sat down with his

sons and daughters and their spouses and explained that whatever was left at his death would be going to Christian ministries. The family said they understood. Afterward his son-in-law took him aside. The young man said, "Thank you—now I know it's really up to me to provide for your daughter."

This young man had believed up until then that anything he did to provide for his family would pale in comparison to what his father-in-law would eventually leave them. Suddenly, he was exactly where God wanted him—in the primary position of responsibility for his family.

Is it really God's money, or does it belong to our children?

Many people have expressed shock when they've heard me say that Christian parents should seriously consider leaving the bulk of their estate to churches, parachurch ministries, missions, and other Kingdom purposes. But that advice comes from decades of not only studying Scripture but also observing what happens when large inheritances are passed on to those who did nothing to earn them. That's why Jesus answered this questioner as he did: "'Teacher, tell my brother to divide the inheritance with me.' . . . [Jesus warns him] 'Watch out! Be on your guard against all kinds of greed; a man's life does not consist in the abundance of his possessions'" (Luke 12:13, 15, NIV).

Of course, if children and grandchildren have

special needs, parents can leave money to them as seems best. But, generally, leaving only a modest portion—enough to help grandchildren with college, for instance—encourages our adult children to work hard, plan, not overspend, and experience the joy of trusting God.

Consider this question: What would you think if your money manager died and left all your money to *his* children? Well, if our money really belongs to God and we are his money managers, what makes us think that when we die it should all go to *our* children, even when they don't need it?

Nanci and I chose to share some of our assets with our grown children when they most needed it—by helping with their down payments on homes. The amount left for them later, when they won't need it, won't be large. We have explained this to them. They know we love them, and they understand that we desire both to honor God *and* to act in their best interests.

When people talk about leaving a large inheritance to their adult children, I ask them if those children really need more money. Nearly always, they reply, "No."

Then I ask, "Since they don't need it, what do you hope your children will do with the money you leave them?"

"Well, it would be great if they gave it away to missions and helping the poor."

"But since God has entrusted the money to you, not them, and since giving it away is what you believe is right, then why don't *you* give it away?"

What's the difference between giving money now and leaving it to good causes when we die?

Passages relating to reward indicate that rewards in Heaven are given for acts of faith we actually do while on Earth. Leaving instructions for what *others* are to do with money that once was ours is not the same as giving it away while we're still here. Death isn't your best opportunity to give; it's the end of your opportunity to give. After all, "it is appointed for men to die once, but after this the judgment" (Hebrews 9:27, NKJV).

Would Jesus have so highly commended the poor widow's offering if she had died that day and bequeathed those two coins to the Temple? Or would he have been so moved if Zacchaeus had said that he would put in his will that the poor should receive half of his estate and he would designate that people he'd cheated be paid back four times over from what he left behind? I don't think so. Sure, it would be good to distribute an estate into God's work, but their reward wouldn't have been comparable, because their actions wouldn't have required faith or sacrifice.

Giving is *voluntarily* parting with an asset. We have no choice but to leave money behind when we die, so designating where it goes, though wise, is *not* sacrificial.

Jesus didn't say to the rich young man, "Leave your estate to the poor when you die." He told him to sell his possessions and give to the poor (Matthew 19:21). This was far more difficult.

I'm convinced that as Christians we need a major

paradigm shift in this area. I believe God desires his money managers not to follow the culture's lead in heaping more wealth upon adult children who don't need it and will likely suffer from receiving it.

And while we will all leave something behind when we die, New Testament principles and examples suggest we shouldn't strive to leave a large estate. John Wesley made a great deal of money on his books, as well as some hymns—about £50,000 in all. Yet at his death his estate was worth only £28.

Wesley was left with so little, not because of poor planning but good planning—he had generously given it to the cause of Christ. Wesley's stated goal was to have as little left as possible when he died. At the end of his life, he wrote in his journal, "I have left no money to anyone in my will, because I had none." What a contrast to Christians who die with vast estates that could have been invested in the Kingdom all along as God provided the assets!

Wouldn't it be fitting for most of us to leave the greatest bulk of our estates to helping the poor, needy, disabled, and oppressed and evangelizing and discipling people all over the world?

In AD 390, John Chrysostom said this to Christian parents: "If you wish to leave much wealth to your children, leave them in God's care. Do not leave them riches, but virtue and skill."

Many of the world's wealthy have left their children huge inheritances but dismal heritages. On the other hand, countless Christians have left their children small material inheritances but a godly heritage of character and spiritual values.

Many adult children who receive a huge financial inheritance end up resenting their parents. Most adult children who receive a great spiritual heritage praise God for their parents.

Passing the Baton of Wise Stewardship

CHAPTER 21

In the Family: Teaching Children How to Manage God's Money and Possessions

EVERYTHING LEARNED IN LIFE, from coping methods to table manners, is learned in families. Families are the heart and soul of society, with the home, not the school, as the primary place of learning. Home is where character is built, habits are developed, and destinies are forged. Proverbs tells us, "Direct your children onto the right path, and when they are older, they will not leave it" (Proverbs 22:6).

Children imitate everything we do, whether important or unimportant, healthy or unhealthy. Sometimes our children will fail to listen to us. Rarely will they fail to imitate us.

Moses told God's people, "You must commit yourselves wholeheartedly to these commands that I am giving you today. Repeat them again and again to your children. Talk about them when you are at home and when you are on the road, when you are going to bed and when you are getting up. Tie them to your hands and wear them on your forehead as reminders. Write them on the doorposts of your house and on your gates" (Deuteronomy 6:6-9).

This great passage describes the training process as both formal and informal. We are constantly to teach our children God's Word and talk about its principles as occasions arise throughout the day. Often, the informal discussions will open a door for the formal instruction, and vice versa.

Every experience your children have with money is a teaching opportunity. Some lessons they will learn the hard way. Children who lose or ruin their favorite possession through carelessness will learn a valuable lesson. So will those who see the joy in another's eyes as a result of them giving something away. Often, parents can help by verbalizing a lesson.

We have no idea how deeply we affect our children by our casual, offhand comments. One night, when one of my daughters was seven years old, she prayed, "Dear Lord, I thank you so much that we are not too rich or too poor." This pleased me but also surprised me—where did it come from? As I thought about it, I remembered that probably six months earlier I had shared briefly with her a verse in Proverbs: "Give me neither poverty nor riches" (Proverbs 30:8). I applied it to a situation we saw while driving somewhere. I had long since forgotten that conversation. Obviously, my daughter hadn't.

The more children have witnessed wise stewardship practiced by their parents, the more natural it will seem to them. If parents give generously, save rather than borrow, and spend carefully, they grant their children a wonderful gift—and help protect them from financial disaster.

How can we help children connect money with work?

As parents, we should teach our children to associate money with labor. Money and possessions do not fall out of the sky; they are earned through diligence and effort. A common mistake that parents make is to dole out money to children arbitrarily. This teaches them to believe money comes easily or automatically. They begin imagining it's their right to have money even when they haven't worked for it—and many carry this misconception into their adult lives.

Although money should be associated with work, not all work should be associated with money. Children shouldn't always be paid for their chores. However, there are many "extras" that can legitimately be rewarded financially, and children can take on jobs outside the home as they grow older, including washing cars, mowing lawns, cleaning house, or babysitting.

Teaching our children a productive work ethic is essential. It's equally important that children learn to correctly prioritize work and other commitments. Young people who are encouraged or allowed by their parents to put other pursuits above ministry, fellowship, and the teaching of Scripture will live out those same principles as adult church members—if they aren't too busy making money to go to church at all.

How can we teach children to save?

Children learn the value of money and the discipline of self-control through saving. They need reasons and incentives to save. If they want a major item, help them develop a plan to work for and save the money. If they stick with their plan to save over a long period of time, buying that item won't be an impulsive decision.

Many parents know what it's like to have teenagers go to costly school events. Kids may want to buy expensive dresses or rent tuxedos and go to fancy restaurants. Parents who automatically pick up the tab for such events do their children a disservice. If teenagers believe that these events warrant that kind of money, they need to work for it themselves—months in advance, if necessary. When working for something is the only alternative, it's amazing how many creative options young people can come up with and still have a great time!

We helped put our daughters through college, just as our parents helped us. However, I don't believe that parents should automatically pay for their children's entire college education. When young people work to earn money for college, they develop character and financial responsibility.

Some parents offer to pay for the classes their children earn As and Bs in, but the student has to pay for any classes in which he or she gets a C or lower. Suddenly they have motivation to study!

How can we help children become generous givers?

We should be raising up givers, not keepers. But the next generation is growing up in the midst of vast wealth, which many will inherit. Yet many have not learned the habits and joys of giving (or the disciplines of saving and wise spending). If we don't teach our children how to give and manage God's money, who will?

- "Train a child in the way he should go, and when he is old he will not turn from it" (Proverbs 22:6, NIV).
- "I have chosen him, so that he will direct his children and his household after him to keep the way of the LORD by doing what is right and just" (Genesis 18:19, NIV).
- "What we have heard and known, what our fathers have told us. We will not hide them from their children; we will tell the next generation the praiseworthy deeds of the LORD, his power, and the wonders he has done" (Psalm 78:3-4, NIV).

If you had no other reason for giving, doing it for your children would be reason enough! Breaking the bonds of materialism in your life—through generous giving and moderate lifestyle choices—will prove to be one of the greatest gifts you can give your children.

Many people who want their children to develop

hearts for God overlook the one thing that Jesus explicitly says will move our children's hearts toward Heaven: giving. Children who are not taught to give—by their parents' example, family discussions, and personal guidance—are hamstrung in their ability to live for Christ. Remember, Jesus taught that our hearts follow whatever we treasure (Matthew 6:21).

The next generation must be shown the joy of giving and taught the discipline of giving. In order to enhance their giving, they must also be taught to avoid debt and control spending. Our duty to our children is clear: "Bring them up in the training and instruction of the Lord" (Ephesians 6:4, NIV).

Some say we shouldn't require our children to give. I disagree. That advice makes no more sense to me than to say, "Don't make your children wash their hands before a meal or wear coats on a cold, windy day."

For those who say, "But giving must be from the heart, not imposed by someone else," I'd respond, "But giving is also a habit, and like all good habits it can and should be cultivated." There's no better way for a parent to cultivate giving than by deliberately making it one of the family's standard practices.

In the movie *Chariots of Fire*, Olympian Eric Liddell says, "I believe God made me for a purpose . . . and when I run, I feel his pleasure." When they give, our children can learn to feel God's pleasure by feeling our pleasure. We should praise our children for giving and resist any temptation to hold them back.

How can we help young children handle money?

We taught our daughters from the earliest age to give a minimum of 10 percent. No matter where their income came from, even as a gift, 10 percent was set aside for the Lord.

Of course, keeping to a routine is no guarantee of spirituality. But the holy habit of giving is like the holy habits of Bible study, prayer, witnessing, and hospitality. Those raised without these habits are at a great disadvantage trying to develop them as adults.

When the girls were seven and five, I gave each of them three jars I'd labeled with the designations "Giving," "Saving," and "Spending." I told them that every time they earned their salary (which was then one dollar per week), they were first to put at least 10 percent into the giving jar, then distribute the rest between the other two jars as they wished. But once they put money in the giving jar, even beyond the tithe (often they would put in 30 percent, sometimes more), it was dedicated to the Lord.

Once they put money in "Saving," they weren't to take it out and spend it except for some upcoming special expenditure. However, they were free to transfer money from saving or spending to giving, or from spending to saving.

I will never forget the night I explained this new system to my daughters. They were so excited they immediately took the money they already had and distributed it between the jars. This simple system probably resulted in more financial education than anything else Nanci and I did.

What can families do together to learn good stewardship?

In chapter 7, on battling materialism in the family, I recommend taking a family field trip to the local dump. I also encourage getting involved together in special missions projects. Family members can work with each other to financially support, pray for, and correspond with a missionary, a needy family, or an orphan. Photos can be posted prominently, and prayers can be offered at dinner or family devotions. Becoming aware of needs elsewhere reminds our children of the opportunity to share our abundance with others.

If you're planning a major family vacation, why not visit a mission field? Combine fun with education by visiting and encouraging church missionary families (provided it benefits the missionaries, too).

An effective way to teach children how to properly spend money is to show them how you spend it. One technique is to bring home an entire paycheck in one dollar bills (explain *that* to the bank teller). Or you could use play money equivalent to your take-home pay to give the same illustration. Put the money in piles to show how much goes to what expenses monthly. This allows children to visualize everything. It helps them compare what's expensive and what isn't, what's a priority and what's not. Some things will surprise children, and they may ask you tough questions. You may reevaluate your budget and make some healthy changes.

How can we teach children self-control?

Few things we can teach our children are more valuable than the discipline of saying no. We must model delayed gratification and teach the discipline of avoiding expenditures when the money could accomplish a higher purpose by being given away, saved, or used more wisely.

Self-control is one of the highest Christian virtues (Galatians 5:22-23; Titus 2:1-12). Sometimes we have to wait longer than we want—but that's what builds our character and self-control. Children need help to develop sales resistance. Every time we say no to our children about candy or a new toy, we can teach them something important.

Children raised this way will usually follow the same pattern of decision making when they're on their own. Those who learn to say no to unnecessary purchases are much more likely to say no to immorality, alcohol, drugs, or shoplifting.

Obviously, parents should sometimes say yes to our children's requests! In the context of good stewardship, giving to our children can teach the lesson of generosity. Tightfisted stinginess is as negative a model as overindulgence. Our goal isn't to be penny-pinchers obsessed with money, but joyful, responsible, and generous stewards of God's abundance.

How can we help children develop good spending habits?

Children can learn to shop intelligently, not buying the first thing they see. I suggest less shopping for entertainment. It can breed discontent to look at all the latest things we don't need and can't afford. Instead, take a family field trip to a shopping center for one specific purpose: Look at all the different things, then ask your children which is really worth the cost in light of what else could be done with the money, especially if invested in God's Kingdom.

As I suggested earlier, you can teach children how to properly spend money by showing them how you spend it. (If you aren't spending it wisely, this could motivate you to change!) By the time children are ten, in some cases younger, they're old enough to be let in on the family budget.

Your children may see things from a money manager's perspective for the first time. Children who've been told to turn off the lights when they leave a room or to shut the front door behind them suddenly understand when they see the stack of money required to pay the electric bill. Children hear their parents' words, but until they can visualize what they mean, words don't sink in.

How can we help children learn greater responsibility?

As parents, our ultimate purpose isn't simply to give our children food and shelter for the first twenty years of life. Our purpose is to one day present to the Lord, the church, and the world mature young adults who are good servants, stewards, and citizens.

As children grow up, they should gradually be weaned financially. By the time they're ten, most children might have their own savings accounts. By twelve, they might have part-time summer jobs. By seventeen, they might be paying for their transportation, recreation, and clothing. Of course, scenarios will vary according to family needs, preferences, work opportunities, and a child's development.

After they complete high school, as long as children are still in their early twenties—especially if they're continuing in school—it may be reasonable to provide their food and lodging. But we must discern when this stops being healthy. The goal is to help our children become increasingly independent of us—which should lead to an increasing dependence on the Lord.

Should we help children learn the hard way?

Children learn by experience. Consequently, Nanci and I occasionally allowed our daughters to make poor financial decisions by spending impulsively. This was difficult for me. But if parents always say no to unwise decisions, even though children may reluctantly obey, they won't learn wisdom through firsthand experience.

When we occasionally began letting our girls buy certain things they wanted, they started learning the hard way. When something of true value came along, they couldn't afford to buy it.

We must be careful not to bail out our children by saying, "I guess you learned your lesson, so I'll get you what you want." If we can keep ourselves from interfering with the natural laws of life, mistakes can be our children's finest teachers. If a twelve-year-old squanders his lunch money, what should his parents do? Nothing. He must earn more money, use the money he's saved, or go without lunch. The lessons of life are very simple and effective—if we will just stay out of the way!

Suppose your child wants a brand-new bicycle like his friends have. One way to teach him the cost of having nice things is to tell him that if he really wants it, you'll loan him the money at the going rate of interest. Work out a payment schedule with him, showing him how much this bicycle will actually cost him and how long it will take to pay it off.

At this point, he may back out of the deal. But if he doesn't, let him go ahead. By the time he pays off the debt from miscellaneous chores—perhaps as much as six months down the road—he will never forget the cost of borrowing.

How can we help children learn to share their possessions?

Sometimes parents are embarrassed by their children's displays of greed and possessiveness. Yet too often we don't provide a model for sharing. What do our children learn when they don't see us sharing our possessions freely? Or when they hear us complain that we loaned someone our car and it was returned dirty or dented? If we view our assets as really belonging to God, we'll respond differently.

Hospitality is one of the strongest ways we can teach our children. By opening our homes to others and being gracious hosts and hostesses, our children see firsthand the value of encouraging other people and drawing close through unselfishly sharing possessions.

How can we help children become thankful?

"Praise the LORD, O my soul, and forget not all his benefits" (Psalm 103:2, NIV). As parents we can lead the way by openly expressing our thankfulness to God and by being careful not to nullify this by complaining when things don't go our way.

We often asked our daughters at night to identify a number of things they were thankful for that day. At first this may be difficult, but in time it develops a sensitive eye to the ways God cares for us. At the top of this list of things to be thankful for is God himself, our loving Redeemer. Next are the family and friends and church he's given us.

Children can also give thanks for material things, for more than just toys—for a body that works, a bed to sleep in, a house to live in, for the air, sunshine, rain. Giving thanks for all these things draws their hearts not to the things themselves but to the One who graciously provides them.

How can we leave a legacy of godly stewardship?

Nothing will interfere more with our children's relationship with God—or even prevent them from having a relationship—than a life centered on things. Our greatest legacy to our children is to help them develop their spiritual lives, their hearts for God.

Although many parents seem content to leave their children a big inheritance, the bigger and better job is to leave them a legacy of wisdom and generosity. They can then pass on this legacy to their own children and their children's children. Godly generations and an eternal impact can result from our simple acts of faithful stewardship. For we are stewards not just of God's money, but of the children he entrusts to our care.

CHAPTER 22

In the Church: Cultivating a Culture of Stewardship and Giving

How do we teach others about stewardship and giving?

Pastors should model and teach a biblical pattern of stewardship. Ezra, spiritual leader of his people, "determined to study and obey the Law of the LORD and to teach those decrees and regulations to the people" (Ezra 7:10).

Ask your pastors to address stewardship and giving from the pulpit. Most pastors know this subject is important but feel self-conscious addressing it on their own initiative. They typically welcome such an invitation.

Fellow Christians ought to disciple each other in financial stewardship. Small groups and Sunday school classes need to discuss it. Those who've learned the hard way about the bondage of debt need to warn others. Young believers need to hear their elders tell how God has used wise money management and giving in their families and of the freedom and joy it has brought.

Husbands and wives should be encouraged to discuss and act on these truths. Because this is one issue in which God invites us to test him, ask God to prove himself. Some wives whose unbelieving husbands resist giving money to God's work have labored creatively to find more ways to cut family spending in order to finance the giving. They have been respectfully persistent about giving, even if at lower levels than they'd prefer, but because of their own sacrificial efforts to find money to give, it hasn't been a divisive issue. In some cases, their heart for following Christ has served to draw their partner to God.

What resources are available to help people become wiser stewards?

I'm grateful that churches, ministries, and Bible studies have made extensive use of my large book *Money, Possessions, and Eternity*, as well as my small book *The Treasure Principle*. (A group study DVD is available at www.epm.org/TPstudydvd.) I wrote *Managing God's Money* to serve as a small and inexpensive resource that covers a lot of ground in addressing financial stewardship with an eternal perspective. The chapters can be easily discussed in a group.

Crown Financial Ministries offers a variety of stewardship Bible studies for churches (www.crown.org). Good Sense Ministry (www.goodsenseministry.com) offers printed and DVD resources by Dick Towner and others, including *Freed-Up Financial Living*. Dave

Ramsey's Financial Peace University has helped many people get out of debt (www.daveramsey.com/fpu/). See Howard Dayton's Compass: Finances God's Way at www.compass1.org. Many families have benefited from the practical financial advice of Ellie Kay (www.elliekay.com).

On the subject of giving, see the excellent online resources of Generous Giving, an organization that offers extensive articles, audio recordings, and videos in addition to outstanding conferences (www.generousgiving.org). Generous Giving's sister organization is Giving Wisely, designed to help people understand when and how to give most strategically (www.givingwisely.com).

Excellence in Giving helps philanthropists maximize the impact of their giving (www.excellenceingiving.org). You'll also find good insights and resources at these locations: www.revolutioningenerosity.com, www.stewardshipministries.org, www.kluth.org, and www.generositymonk.com.

The National Christian Foundation has helped thousands of people give to ministries they believe in (www.nationalchristian.com). Ron Blue's Kingdom Advisors assists Christian financial advisors in taking an active role in counseling their clients toward investing more in God's Kingdom (www.kingdomadvisors.org).

I taught a class called "A Theology of Money" that deals with many of the subjects I address in this book. The twelve one-hour sessions are available on DVD or can be downloaded from our Web site (www.epm.org/moneyclass).

I've compiled a list of outstanding books and other resources on stewardship and giving, available at www.epm.org/moneybooks.

I know of entire churches that have been transformed by preaching and teaching and encouraging small group discussions based on the Bible and Christian books on stewardship and giving. Such studies can touch countless individuals. I've received many e-mails in which people tell beautiful stories of changed lives and new joy, freedom, and Kingdom impact.

Despite the availability of many good materials, according to the Christian Stewardship Association, only 10 percent of churches have active programs to teach biblical financial and stewardship principles. Only 15 percent of pastors say they have been equipped by their denomination or seminary to teach biblical financial principles. Only 2 to 4 percent of seminaries offer courses, seminars, or Bible studies to teach stewardship principles, and only 1 to 2 percent of Christian colleges offer such training.

I encourage Bible colleges, Christian liberal arts colleges, and seminaries to develop courses centered on a biblical theology of stewardship and giving. We need much more than a class on budgeting and financial planning. We need a Bible-based, Christ-centered theology of money and possessions that tackles critical stewardship issues pertaining to all Christians.

In churches, financial stewardship should not be

viewed as just one among many competing "special interests," occasionally offered as an elective. Managing God's money is a central biblical subject of extreme importance. It's needed most by those least prone to take the initiative to be trained in it. Financial stewardship should be unapologetically addressed by Christian leaders, who are called upon to declare "the whole counsel of God" to the people he entrusts to their care (Acts 20:27, ESV).

If we fail to teach biblical stewardship and radical generosity in our churches, why should we be surprised that so few Christians appear to be practicing them?

Is there a right time and place to tell our stewardship and giving stories?

Jesus told us never to give in order to be seen by others (Matthew 6:1). Yet maybe ten minutes earlier in the same sermon, he said, "You are the light of the world—like a city on a hilltop that cannot be hidden. No one lights a lamp and then puts it under a basket. Instead, a lamp is placed on a stand, where it gives light to everyone in the house. In the same way, *let your good deeds shine out for all to see, so that everyone will praise your heavenly Father*" (Matthew 5:14-16).

Jesus commands us to let our good deeds shine so everyone can see them. Why? So everyone will praise God, *not* us! In other words, there is a way to talk about every good deed, including giving, that does not involve self-praise but instead brings praise to God and illumination and encouragement to others.

Every church has wise and generous managers of God's money who have a great deal to teach others. When people hear stories of the freedom experienced through getting out of debt, they are often inspired to make similar positive changes. They may go to those who told their stories and seek counsel and mentoring.

Ask people at your church if they can point out prayer warriors. Most can. Now ask them to point out *giving warriors*, people who have chosen a modest debt-resistant lifestyle so they can give away 100 percent above that to God's Kingdom. The fact that the term *giving warrior* isn't in our vocabulary says it all, doesn't it?

As high-jump teammates raise the bar for each other, shouldn't we raise the bar of stewardship and giving and provide growing Christians with something to strive for? The writer to the Hebrews challenges us: "Let us think of ways to motivate one another to acts of love and good works" (Hebrews 10:24).

Studies show we are doing very poorly in passing on the stewardship and giving baton to the next generation. In fact, the younger church people are, the lower the percentage they give to God. I think a large part of the reason is that we older Christians have failed to model an attractive and compelling lifestyle of good stewardship and generous giving.

We need to pass on to faithful people what God has graciously taught us over the years about money management, so that they might be able to teach others what they learn from us (2 Timothy 2:2).

Surely we shouldn't hide joyful obedience and growth in basic areas of discipleship. If we do, it's predictable that the church won't learn to pray, study, witness, parent, manage money, or give. If we are committed to silence about spiritual disciplines, we'll never be able to hear from those to whom God has shown great grace. No light will shine, no one will see good deeds, and no one will glorify the Father in Heaven.

By spotlighting testimonies involving every spiritual discipline *except* giving, we fail to mentor people *in* giving. "As you excel in everything—in faith, in speech, in knowledge, in all earnestness, and in our love for you—*see that you excel in this act of grace also*" (2 Corinthians 8:7, ESV).

People respond best when they have tangible examples they can follow in their leaders and their peers. How does a young Christian in the church learn to give? Where can she go to see what giving looks like in the life of a believer captivated by Christ? Why are we surprised when, seeing no other example, she takes her cues from a materialistic society?

To turn the tide of materialism in the Christian community, we desperately need bold and accessible models—mentors in Kingdom-centered living.

It would have been an incalculable loss to my spiritual life as a young believer if I hadn't heard the stories of Hudson Taylor, George Müller, Amy Carmichael, and R. G. LeTourneau. They lived to please God. Reading and hearing about what God did in them inspired me to ask him to stretch and use me through increasing my giving to God.

By all means let's be careful to avoid self-praise. But let's not fail to testify to God's gracious empowerment as we seek to influence others in the liberating journey of faithful stewardship and joyful giving.

What can we do now to prepare ourselves for our coming job evaluation?

We can avoid later judgment by God through examining and correcting ourselves now: "If we would examine ourselves, we would not be judged by God in this way" (1 Corinthians 11:31).

Tolstoy said, "The antagonism between life and conscience may be removed in two ways: by a change of life or by a change of conscience." Many of us have elected to adjust our consciences rather than our lives. Our powers of rationalization allow us to live in luxury and indifference while others, whom we could help if we chose to, go hungry, are abused and exploited, or go to Hell.

If we fear appearing foolish by taking seriously the New Testament view of money and possessions, we should remind ourselves of what the Bible says about being fools for Christ (1 Corinthians 1:18-31; 4:8-13). Better to be seen as fools now in the eyes of other people—including other Christians—than to be seen as fools forever in the eyes of an audience of One whose judgment is the only one that will ultimately matter.

Money Management and an Eternal Investment Mentality

GOD LOVES A cheerful giver, and he loves a faithful steward. When God is happy with our management of his money, we will be happy. When God is not happy with what we do with his money, we will be unhappy. Why? Because God's children are made to find joy in pleasing him.

Have you transferred the title deed to God?

From the beginning of this book I've sought to make clear that we will never manage God's money well unless we *truly* believe it *is* God's money.

God owns all things, whether or not we recognize it. He already owns the title deed of the whole universe, not just our little part of it. Nevertheless, God calls upon us to relinquish what we've imagined was ours and give it to him. Life becomes much clearer—and in some respects much easier—when we abandon the false god of our ownership and authority, which manifests itself in a deadly spirit of entitlement. That spirit, in turn, leads us to believe that the universe should operate according to our preferences and that we have grounds for complaint when it doesn't (which is most of the time).

There is a difference between *believing* God owns everything and cheerfully *submitting* to his ownership of everything. This is why I recommend deliberately transferring the title deed of ourselves and all our assets to God.

Have you invited him to be what Scripture says he is—Creator, Owner, and Controller of you, your family, and "your" money and possessions? Have you extended the invitation again after you've forgotten and taken things back into your own hands?

A test of our stewardship is whether we ask God to show us what to do with his money. If we don't consult him, no matter what we say, we're behaving as if we were owners, not stewards.

When I grasp that I'm a steward, not an owner, it totally changes my perspective. Suddenly, I'm not asking, "How much of my money shall I, out of the goodness of my heart, give to God?" Rather, I'm asking, "Since all of 'my' money is really yours, Lord, how would you like me to invest your money today?"

To visualize and reinforce this vital concept in your mind, I suggest you sit down and draw up a title deed, or use the one that follows. Married couples may wish to do this together. It can be a healthy statement of joyful surrender to God and his lordship.

⊰ TITLE DEED ⊱

Date: _____

I hereby acknowledge God's ownership of me and all "my" money and possessions, as well as everything else I've ever imagined I own—including my family and loved ones.

Instead of seeing myself as the ultimate recipient, I will see myself as God's delivery person. I will enjoy what he intends me to keep and cheerfully let go of what he intends me to share or give away.

From this point forward, I will think of all these assets as his to do with as he wishes. I will ask God to help me understand the Bible's instruction about stewardship and how he wishes me to manage and invest his assets to further his Kingdom.

I realize this will mean surrendering some temporary treasures and downsizing my earthly kingdom. In doing so, I will upsize God's Kingdom and gain eternal treasures. This will decrease my worry and guilt and increase my eternal perspective, joy, and contentment, and deepen my love for Jesus, my Savior and King. I do this for his glory and the good of all.

Signed:_____

Witness:_____

Has God strategically entrusted his assets to you for this time and place?

The fact that you're reading these words is probably part of God's plan to change your life—and in turn, to shape history and eternity.

Sound like an overstatement? It's not. Remember what Mordecai said to Esther: "If you remain silent at this time, relief and deliverance for the Jews will arise from another place, but you and your father's family will perish. And who knows but that you have come to royal position for such a time as this?" (Esther 4:14, NIV).

Esther was in a position of privilege, so is nearly everyone reading this book. Do you have some education, and are you literate? Do you have food, clothing, shelter, a car, and some electronic equipment? Then you are among the privileged, the world's truly wealthy.

One ministry calls a group of its key donors "History's Handful." Is there an exaggerated sense of significance in this term? I don't think so. Giving to God's great causes is a calling and a privilege that should infuse us not with self-importance but with a sense of destiny.

It's no accident that you live in this time and place in history. Why has God entrusted you with wealth? For such a time as this: "Your plenty will supply what they need. . . . You will be made rich in every way so that you can be generous on every occasion" (2 Corinthians 8:14; 9:11, NIV).

What is the spiritual gift of giving, and who has it?

In his infinite wisdom, God grants to his children spiritual gifts—supernatural endowments of the Holy Spirit—empowering his people to bring help to others and a sense of fulfillment to themselves. And with these gifts he provides resources so that we can exercise them.

In Romans 12, Paul lists seven spiritual gifts, including serving, teaching, mercy, leadership, and giving. "In his grace, God has given us different gifts for doing certain things well. . . . If your gift is to encourage others, be encouraging. *If it is giving, give generously.* If God has given you leadership ability, take the responsibility seriously. And if you have a gift for showing kindness to others, do it gladly" (Romans 12:6-8).

As a young Christian, I was taught about the spiritual gifts and had long conversations with many people about numbers of gifts. Yet I don't recall a single presentation on or discussion concerning the gift of giving. It never occurred to me what it might look like or whether God might have given it to me.

Of course, all of us are called to serve, show mercy, and give, even if we don't have those specific gifts. But I believe that in different times of history, God has sovereignly distributed certain gifts more widely (such as the gift of mercy during devastating plagues and the gift of teaching during the Reformation).

Suppose God wanted to fulfill his world evangelization plan and help an unprecedented number of suffering people. What gifts might you expect him to distribute widely? Wouldn't one of them be the gift of giving? Since God provides resources appropriate to each gift, what might you expect him to provide for those with the gift of giving? Substantial material resources. Isn't that exactly what he has done? (The question is, What have *we* done with what he has provided?)

If God has given you a good income and plentiful resources, isn't this a likely indication that he has given you the gift of giving? Are you learning to exercise your gift, just as those with the gift of teaching or mercy or leadership should be learning to exercise theirs?

How do we learn to teach or lead or give? *We learn by doing.*

We become givers by giving.

God has given most of us, I believe, several spiritual gifts. Someone asked me, if I had to give up other gifts and keep only one, which would it be? My answer was, "The gift of giving." No other gift has brought me more joy. Yet I am convinced that the gift of giving remains suppressed because it is so seldom acknowledged and so many who have it haven't yet exercised it, remaining ignorant of its exquisite joys and rewards.

Are we in danger of overemphasizing giving?

You've probably noticed that while I've dealt with many aspects of stewardship, I've never strayed too far from giving. Whenever someone says, "There's a lot more to financial stewardship than giving," I always agree. But I point out that while stewardship involves much more than giving, it never involves less than giving.

I've been warned not to emphasize giving. I'm told it might lead to extremes, and people might start neglecting the material needs of their families. When I look at my life and others', however, I see little danger of that!

Do we *really* believe we'll stand before Christ's judgment seat and hear him say, "I have this against you—you gave too much; you should have kept more for yourself and your family!" Jesus never called someone a fool for giving too much and keeping too little. But, in the parable about the rich man, he *did* call someone a fool for keeping too much and giving too little (Luke 12:20-21).

Many people's philosophy of finances seems to be, "As long as I have it, why not spend it?" A more biblical philosophy would be, "As long as I have it, why not give it?" The burden of proof should fall on spenders, not givers. For we who already have plenty, when we receive more, shouldn't it be our default setting to give?

Have you ever played one of those card games where the winner is the one who runs out of cards first? At the end of the game, every card left counts against you. The American dream is to die with as many cards in your hand as possible. Perhaps we're playing the wrong game.

How seriously will we take what Jesus said?

Jesus made some pretty radical statements about money:

> If you are faithful in little things, you will
> be faithful in large ones. But if you are
> dishonest in little things, you won't be
> honest with greater responsibilities. And if
> you are untrustworthy about worldly wealth,
> who will trust you with the true riches of
> heaven? And if you are not faithful with
> other people's things, why should you be
> trusted with things of your own? No one can
> serve two masters. . . . You cannot serve both
> God and money. (Luke 16:10-13)

After he said this, "the Pharisees, who dearly loved their money, heard all this and scoffed at him" (verse 14). The Pharisees were the religious conservatives of their day. The lesson for us is that we may believe the Scriptures, defend them, be willing to die for them, and still be money lovers who reject and take offense at the radical teachings of Christ about money and possessions.

Let's just admit the obvious: The New Testament call to discipleship, compassion, and giving bears no resemblance to the way many of us think about and handle money. It's time to get beyond the theoretical "I'd be willing to give up anything if God asked me to" and start actually giving things away in order to do what he has commanded us.

For some of us, it's time to beg God's forgiveness for our self-indulgent lifestyles, our indifference to human need, and our shortsightedness about eternity. For others, it's time to joyfully move forward and raise the bar higher. It's time for all of us to live a life of obedient and exhilarating discipleship. It's time to say no to the American dream and yes to the Kingdom dreams of the risen Christ.

What Will You Do Now?

A MAN WHO owns a profitable business read my book *The Treasure Principle* and told me that for the first time he knows why God has blessed him financially. It's not so he can drive nicer cars and live in a bigger house. It's to build God's Kingdom. I told him about a dozen different missions groups, pro-life projects, prison ministries, and ways to help persecuted Christians, and he was moved by all the wonderful investment options. He finished our conversation determined to liquidate more assets to dramatically expand his eternal investment portfolio. I wish you could have heard the freedom and excitement in his voice. He's thrilled to have finally gotten on board with what matters!

I invite you to join this brother in joyfully leveraging the assets that God has entrusted to you. Make an eternal difference. Send your treasures on to Heaven where they'll safely await you. When you do, you'll feel the freedom and sense the smile of God.

God tells us to prepare for the long tomorrow by

using our short todays to exchange Earthly treasures for Heavenly ones. In eternity, we'll worship God with people of every tribe, nation, and language. We'll thank each other for acts of faithfulness done for Christ while we lived on Earth. We'll tell each other our stories, enjoying the warmth and sharing the joy with our Lord as the center of attention. What a privilege! Do you have trouble getting out of bed in the morning? If picturing such scenes in Heaven doesn't give you a purpose for living, I don't know what will!

Nothing is more fleeting than the moment of conviction. If we turn our backs on that moment, the next moment may not come until we stand before our Lord. We dare not procrastinate. May what will be most important to us five minutes after we die become most important to us now.

As believers in Christ, our theology gives us perspective. It tells us that this life is the preface—not the book. It's the preliminaries—not the main event.

Listen to these words of our Savior: "If any of you wants to be my follower, you must turn from your selfish ways, take up your cross, and follow me. If you try to hang on to your life, you will lose it. But if you give up your life for my sake and for the sake of the Good News, you will save it. And what do you benefit if you gain the whole world but lose your own soul? Is anything worth more than your soul?" (Mark 8:34-37).

I think of our lives in terms of a dot and a line signifying two phases. Our present life on Earth is the dot. It begins. It ends. It's brief. However, from the dot, a line extends that goes on forever. That line is eternity, which Christians will spend in Heaven.

Right now we're living in the dot. But what are we living *for*? The person who lives for the dot lives for treasures on Earth that end in junkyards. The person who lives for the line lives for treasures in Heaven that never fade. Faithful stewardship and generous giving are living for the line.

I pray that your heart will be touched and your life forever changed through embracing Scripture's exciting perspectives on being God's money managers. May we spend our remaining time here investing God's money in that eternal Kingdom he's preparing for us, so that a million years from now we'll be grateful that we did. And when we first meet him face-to-face, may we hear him say those incredible words:

"Well done, good and faithful servant. . . . Enter into the joy of your master" (Matthew 25:21, ESV).

If this book has been helpful, Randy Alcorn would enjoy hearing from you on his Facebook page: www.facebook.com/randyalcorn.

You can also connect with Randy and his organization at

www.epm.org
www.epm.org/blog
www.twitter.com/randyalcorn

Eternal Perspective Ministries
39085 Pioneer Blvd., Suite 206
Sandy, OR 97055
503-668-5200

Many of the principles and issues raised in this book are developed in more detail in *Money, Possessions, and Eternity* (Tyndale House, revised 2004), a biblical and practical treatment of financial stewardship. Randy deals specifically with the subject of giving in his little book *The Treasure Principle* (Multnomah, 2001), which has sold over 1.3 million copies.

A six-DVD set of Randy Alcorn teaching twelve one-hour classes on "A Theology of Money" is available from Eternal Perspective Ministries: www.epm.org/moneyclass.

There are many articles related to money and giving on EPM's Web site at www.epm.org/resources/category/money-and-giving.

Acknowledgments

I WANT TO thank Jason Beers for his edits that got me going on this project. Thanks also to Steve Tucker, Doreen Button, Stephanie Anderson, and Kathy Norquist for their editorial suggestions, which were immensely helpful. Thanks to Bonnie Hiestand for her speedy typing of my handwritten notes, as well as some work I assigned her in the manuscript. And many thanks to my new (and first ever) agent, Bill Reeves, who might not have known what he was getting into but whose servant's heart and professional excellence have been a great encouragement to me.

Thanks to the Tyndale House team, many of whom have become good friends, including Ron Beers, Carol Traver, Maria Eriksen, Lisa Jackson, Andrea Lindgren, Erin Gwynne, Dan Farrell, and the entire marketing, sales, and editorial staff who have worked in relationship to my books over the years. I am grateful also for the Christ-centered leadership of Tyndale House provided by Mark Taylor, Jeff Johnson, and Paul Mathews. Finally, many thanks to Stephanie Voiland for her edits at the end of the project.

OTHER BOOKS BY RANDY ALCORN

FICTION

Deadline
Dominion
Deception
Edge of Eternity
Lord Foulgrin's Letters
The Ishbane Conspiracy
Safely Home

NONFICTION

Heaven
Touchpoints: Heaven
50 Days of Heaven
In Light of Eternity
Money, Possessions, and Eternity
The Law of Rewards
ProLife Answers to ProChoice Arguments
Sexual Temptation booklet
The Goodness of God
The Grace and Truth Paradox
The Purity Principle
The Treasure Principle
Why ProLife?
If God Is Good
The Promise of Heaven

KIDS

Heaven for Kids
Wait Until Then
Tell Me About Heaven